Leaders of the Crowd

Adam Gower

Leaders of the Crowd

Conversations with Crowdfunding Visionaries and How Real Estate Stole the Show

Adam Gower
National Real Estate Forum
Beverly Hills, CA, USA

ISBN 978-3-030-00382-1   ISBN 978-3-030-00383-8   (eBook)
https://doi.org/10.1007/978-3-030-00383-8

Library of Congress Control Number: 2018963984

© The Editor(s) (if applicable) and The Author(s), under exclusive licence to Springer Nature Switzerland AG 2018
This work is subject to copyright. All rights are solely and exclusively licensed by the Publisher, whether the whole or part of the material is concerned, specifically the rights of translation, reprinting, reuse of illustrations, recitation, broadcasting, reproduction on microfilms or in any other physical way, and transmission or information storage and retrieval, electronic adaptation, computer software, or by similar or dissimilar methodology now known or hereafter developed.
The use of general descriptive names, registered names, trademarks, service marks, etc. in this publication does not imply, even in the absence of a specific statement, that such names are exempt from the relevant protective laws and regulations and therefore free for general use.
The publisher, the authors and the editors are safe to assume that the advice and information in this book are believed to be true and accurate at the date of publication. Neither the publisher nor the authors or the editors give a warranty, express or implied, with respect to the material contained herein or for any errors or omissions that may have been made. The publisher remains neutral with regard to jurisdictional claims in published maps and institutional affiliations.

Cover image © Richard Gardner / Alamy Stock Photo

This Palgrave Macmillan imprint is published by the registered company Springer Nature Switzerland AG
The registered company address is: Gewerbestrasse 11, 6330 Cham, Switzerland

*To my sons Oliver, Simon, and Felix: the future leaders of the crowd.
Now brush your teeth and go to bed*

Acknowledgments

I had a blast writing this book primarily because it involved having discussions with some of the brightest, most inspirational people in the country: those who have seeded the new industry of real estate crowdfunding—whether it was their intent to or not. Naturally, therefore, I start by thanking those I spoke to for this book and who shared with me their incredible stories: David Weild IV, Jenny Kassan, Dina Ellis Rochkind, Doug Rand, Woodie Neiss, Ben Miller, Eve Picker, Ian Ippolito, Jason Fritton, Jilliene Helman, Harold Hofer, Nav Athwal, and Andy Green. Thanks also to Rod Turner at Manhattan Street Capital for supplying some amazing market data that underscores the dominance of the real estate industry as the primary beneficiary of JOBS Act regulations.

Though it may seem an unlikely facet of writing a book, there were some technical and communication challenges for which I am most grateful to Nichole Elliott, Judy Mahan, and Cory Karpin for their assistance each time I invaded their offices. Thanks to editor Cindy Draughon, and particularly to Sharon Goodman for her detailed feedback on the introduction and conclusion sections when I most needed it. Tula Weis and Jacqueline Young are, as before, great partners who make working with Palgrave Macmillan a tremendous pleasure.

Thanks are also due to my friends for their encouragement, bordering though it sometimes did on disbelief that I should be writing another book: CT Bell for always being prepared to lubricate the wheels of thought with me, Quintin Lever despite his united approach to crowds, and Adam Herz for the courteous epithets with which he always addresses me.

Most of all, thanks Debbie for having the confidence that I will, eventually, get it done, and to Oliver, Simon, and Felix, who will have to read the rest of the book to discover if they are mentioned a third time.

Contents

1	**Introduction**	1
	Chapter Overview	6
2	**Inception: David Weild IV**	13
	The Collapse of Small Cap Liquidity	16
	Thought Leadership	21
3	**The Letter: Jenny Kassan**	27
4	**Advocate: Sherwood Neiss**	33
5	**Senate Lead Staffer: Dina Ellis Rochkind**	45
	On-Ramp, 506(c), Regulation Crowdfunding	51
	Most Impactful Component	53
	The Lobbyists	54
6	**Investor Protections: Andy Green**	57
7	**The White House: Doug Rand**	69
	The Lobbyists	78
	Event Planning	80
	Concerns	81
8	**Rich Uncles: Harold Hofer**	83
	Long-Term JOBS Act Potential	90

9	Fundrise: Ben Miller	93
10	RealtyShares: Nav Athwal	103
11	Investor: Ian Ippolito	115
12	RealtyMogul: Jilliene Helman	125
13	Patch of Land: Jason Fritton	131
14	Small Change: Eve Picker Complicated Finance	143 145
15	Conclusion	153
Glossary		161
Index		165

1

Introduction

Crowdfunding is nothing new; it was prohibited in 1933 as an antidote to the Great Depression and revived in 2012 as a cure for the Great Recession. Indeed, post-civil war America was built on crowdfunding during an era when the entire financial system rested on a foundation of investment from ordinary Americans who could freely invest, without limitation, in anything they wanted to by buying stocks and bonds through syndications—the crowdfunding of the day.

The earliest syndicates were created by the financial institutions that dominated the American landscape. The financial titans of the late nineteenth and early twentieth centuries syndicated the issuance of stocks and bonds to the general public through expansive hierarchies of distribution channels to finance the railroads, the steel industry, and all the infrastructure development in America. Corporate principals and the financiers who assembled the syndicates that provided the necessary capital created deal structures that almost eliminated risk to themselves by pushing it onto the general public. Issuers in America's early crowdfunding landscape hid financial arrangements from public view, manipulated markets, had no limitations on how they advertised, or to whom, or what they did or did not disclose, which meant that those least able to shoulder the burden of risk were those who unwittingly did. Indeed, prior to the Securities Act of 1933, there were no restrictions on how much anyone could invest, how wealthy they were, or what they needed to know before making an investment.

However, this unrestrained marketing of securities by issuers and their consumption by investors contributed to an exuberance for stocks that ended in 1929 with the biggest financial crisis and stock market crash the world had ever seen. To ameliorate the risk of this happening again, policymakers sought to protect investors by regulating how those in need of capital could solicit investment from the general public. Four years after the stock market crash that led to the Great Depression, Congress shut down crowdfunding, passing the Securities Act of 1933. The Act created a sharp dividing line between public and private sectors. Companies could solicit investments in their shares from the general public, but now they were subject to extensive disclosure requirements that ensured they provided everyone with the same information they would were they soliciting all they needed from one influential sophisticated investor. To "go public," issuers would now have to submit to stringent regulations restricting how they advertised and what they said, and would be subject to tight oversight and strict disclosure and reporting requirements.

There were exemptions from these regulations, however. The Act continued to permit capital raising by companies without such onerous restrictions under two conditions. One, a pre-existing relationship was necessary between the person or entity raising the money and the investor; and two, the investor must be wealthy enough to withstand the loss of their investment.

Real estate deal sizes, too small to warrant the kinds of public offerings contemplated by the Securities Act, caused developers to gravitate instead to utilizing the regulatory exemptions, preferring to raise capital only from wealthy investors they already knew. Consequently, as legislators had been primarily focused on restricting investor solicitation by companies and financiers and had not specifically targeted the real estate industry when they passed the 1933 Act, the effect of their actions was to push capital formation in real estate into exclusive private enclaves of wealthy, well-connected investors. As the decades went by, these closed circles became wealthier, and as the cost of real estate development increased, the minimum requirement to invest in a deal increased proportionately, as well. This further distanced those without substantial wealth from the opportunity to participate.

That said, the 1933 Securities Act precipitated a relative calm for financial markets as it was intended to do, and it wasn't until 2008–2009 that the threat of systemic failure once again loomed when stock and real estate markets nearly collapsed and liquidity almost completely dried up. Outdated over time and anachronistic in the Internet age, repercussions of the 1933 Act were being felt by folk in all walks of life and strata of society. In the eyes of some, corporate America had come to dominate every aspect of daily life and small companies and entrepreneurs had little or no access to the capital they needed for growth, squeezed out as they were of mainstream capital markets by a financial elite. They were kept out of public markets because no one was championing their causes to the general public. Entrepreneurs were stymied by regulations generations old that precluded them from going to their own customers to invite them to invest in their companies.

Anxious to resolve the worst financial crisis since the Great Depression, and one that threatened to be just as bad, America's politicians began drawing upon insights from their constituents. The 1933 Securities Act had done its job, they learned, but circumstances nearly 80 years on were different, and the consequences of leaving the Act untouched for so long were beginning to have broad deleterious effects across the economy. This was most starkly thrown into light during the Great Recession that started around 2007. Liquidity had been sucked out of the markets, companies were struggling to regain their economic balance, and legislators were looking for ways to not only bring vigor back to the markets but also step back from the precipice of systemic collapse.

The legislators reflected upon the restrictions laid down in 1933 and, in a variety of different ways, set about writing new deregulatory bills that would facilitate capital formation to make the process more relevant for the time. At the sharp end of the research needed to craft effective legislation were the staff of these politicians; the ones who took input from and advised the advocates and who wrote the bills. These public servants scoured the country for experts in finance and capital formation and the message they heard most clearly and loudly was a demand for crowdfunding. Constituents and experts alike were talking about a financing tool that could leverage the power of the Internet through digital marketing and social media to raise small amounts of capital in large volumes from the masses. Together with their political masters, a coterie of civil servants set about crafting language that would form the foundation upon which bipartisan legislative agreement could be negotiated and agreed upon.

While Congress was busy trying to find ways to bring liquidity through crowdfunding back into the markets to help small companies, some in real estate had been hankering for the opportunity to raise capital from the general public for years. Their motivation was at the same time as prosaic as it was practical; they needed money to capitalize their deals, and they had a keen awareness that those precluded from investing in real estate nevertheless had a strong desire to do so.

These pragmatic visionaries were less concerned about legislative change than they were about the immediate capital challenges they faced every day. Consequently, as legislation started wending its way through the halls of Washington, the real estate voice was not heard; its industry leaders were too busy finding deals and constructing buildings to consider lobbying for regulatory change. Instead, some of them set about finding creative ways to utilize existing regulations to achieve the democratization of real estate investing. They had come up against a bottleneck for raising capital and the pressure was building to find ways beyond the restrictions of the 1933 Act.

A series of unrelated capital formation bills started to gain traction in Congress that ultimately were all tied together to form what was called the JOBS Act, an acronym for Jumpstart Our Business Startups. The most important feature of the new Act was that it dialed back the restrictions laid down in 1933 prohibiting issuers from soliciting people they did not know. This unlocked the door to open advertising to the general public, technically called "general solicitation." In the pre-1933 world, people were typically solicited to buy shares in companies through magazine and newspaper advertisements or through word of mouth via the syndicates and dealer networks that supported the syndicate structures. However, in 2012, advertising meant that while the Internet could be used, it came with the corollary that if anyone wanted to take advantage of the new regulations, all the digital marketing and e-commerce tools using the Internet would have to be learned. For real estate, this gave birth to a brand new industry at the intersection of real estate and tech; one where the ancient, staid world of real estate merged with the latest, fast-moving world of online digital marketing and e-commerce.

When the JOBS Act passed, those real estate leaders who had already been seeking ways to achieve the goals the Act aimed at were the first to recognize the opportunity it presented. What set these early adopters apart is that they recognized the new laws of the JOBS Act would be a boon for real estate finance even though the Act was authored to benefit small companies rather than with real estate in mind. Not only that, every one of them also immediately realized that the opportunity required a sophisticated tech solution. The pioneers of the new tech-enabled real estate finance industry partnered with tech experts who complemented their real estate skills or, in the case of those whose background were in tech, someone who had the real estate skills they lacked.

Their visionary leadership carved a pathway that enabled a completely new industry to emerge; one where companies marrying real estate with technology gave rise to an ecosystem that allowed a host of market places to spring up. Some call these changes revolutionary; others label them transformational.

The change has been no less profound for the general public. For the first time since the 1930s, investors were given the opportunity to invest in deals never before accessible, and they could invest in smaller amounts than ever before, which lent itself to the opportunity to diversify across real estate investments. This alone opened up a new way of investing in real estate never before available; one where investors could put money into a range of asset classes, investment strategies, geographical locations, and sponsors. Sponsors, the person wanting to raise money, suddenly found themselves with a huge potential constituency of investors they could reach out to in a fraction of the time and at a fraction of the cost it used to take.

As with the 1933 Act, real estate was not a target in the sights of the authors of the 2012 Act. What is particularly notable about the real estate visionaries in this book is that they recognized what an incredible game-changer the JOBS Act would be for the industry. They connected the dots and knew its potential for revolutionary impact on their industry. They acted on their instincts and courageously built some of the largest, most influential companies and online investment platforms that became vanguards in a new era of real estate capital formation.

In fact, the new industry they seeded where real estate meets tech has been the single largest beneficiary of the JOBS Act. By 2016, scarcely two years after the rules were promulgated by the Securities and Exchange Commission (SEC) after the Act passed, real estate crowdfunding surpassed $3.5 billion. At time of writing, the companies represented in this book alone have seen a combined total of nearly $10 billion in capitalized real estate projects. Their growth, and that of this new industry, has the classic hockey stick growth curve. Indeed, Forbes projects that total industry volume will reach $300 billion before its tenth year. With over $6 trillion of commercial real estate in the United States today, $66 trillion of untapped accredited investor wealth, and a total of nearly $90 trillion in overall household wealth in America, there remains tremendous room for further growth. While not even considered during the authorship of the JOBS Act as a likely beneficiary, the real estate industry has come to dominate the crowdfunding world.

* * *

This book is not intended to be nor is it a definitive history of the formation of a piece of legislation or the emergence of a new industry. Instead, it tells the story of how the JOBS Act came to be and how real estate capitalized on it by providing the perspective of those *Leaders of the Crowd* who were among the very first pioneers.

These stories were written based on conversations the author had with the participants. You can find more information by going to https://leadersofthecrowd.com/

Chapter Overview

This book describes where the JOBS Act came from and how it impacted the real estate industry. It tells the story by relating the experiences of those leaders who were involved in the genesis of the Act, its authorship, and how it was picked up by the visionaries of the real estate industry. It is structured sequentially, first describing the inception of the Act through how it passed through the halls of power in Washington, to how it was adopted by real estate leaders, whose influence is transforming the industry.

Each chapter in this book has its own style and its own personality corresponding with the leader whose story it tells, relating that story through the lens of their experience. The book is a vignette that describes one man's perspective, the author's, of how the most transformational change to impact the real estate industry in generations was conceived, gestated, and emerged to change real estate capital formation forever.

Following this introductory chapter, Chap. 2, Inception, tells the story of **David Weild IV**, whose insights led to the genesis of the Act. From his lofty perch as Vice Chairman of Nasdaq, Weild started seeing problems with jobs growth stemming from illiquidity and lack of aftermarket support for small cap companies that started in the late 1990s. The irony of what Weild saw was that it was the smallest of financial instruments, the "tick," that was, in fact, creating the largest problems in the market. By reducing the size of the margin a trader could create a commission on, the incentive to sell shares in smaller cap companies was eliminated. This created an implosion in the ecosystem of service providers required to support capital formation for the small and startup companies that needed it the most. Academics have subsequently called this "the ecosystem theory of small IPO decline."

A dominant theme throughout Weild's career, and one that remains acutely in his focus to this day, is that most often the best-intentioned ideas have unintended consequences. The same holds true of the revolution that reduced tick sizes in trading and is what drew him to driving change that ultimately contributed to the development of the JOBS Act.

In Chap. 3, The Letter, lawyer **Jenny Kassan** was seeing an unjust imbalance between the haves and the have-nots, a distinction between those who had access to capital even though they least needed it, and those who didn't have access to capital even though they most needed it. Kassan's pivotal role in the formation of the JOBS Act was sending a letter that catalyzed lawmakers' awareness of capital formation problems at the smaller end of the scale. At the time of her part in the story of how the Act unfolded, Jenny was specializing in securities law, assisting small companies in raising capital for their businesses. Despite having identified a creative methodology within securities law to effectively crowdfund money for her clients, Jenny was frustrated by the complexity and cost restrictions placed on small business owners. Financial markets were dominated by big business and large corporations. Jenny saw an uneven playing field that squeezed out the most important sector of the economy which, as she saw it, was the grassroots of the economy, the 50 percent of companies that received little or no support from Wall Street.

Together with her partners, Jenny sent a letter to the SEC advocating expansion of the exemptions already permitted under the 1933 Securities Act. She contacted as many like-minded people as she could and asked them to express support for her ideas. As a consequence, the SEC received more positive comments for the petition than it had ever received before, elevating the need for change from theory to tangible constituent demand.

Sherwood "Woodie" Neiss, a successful entrepreneur in need of capital, is the Advocate featured in Chap. 4. Neiss wanted to raise money for his startup company by contacting his biggest fans, his customers, and soliciting investment from them. He could not believe that an obscure law written in 1933 prevented him from doing this. It was inconceivable to him that in the Information Age, he was actually prohibited from using the online digital tools commonplace in society to invite his customers, his product's biggest fans, from investing in his company. Not satisfied with the status quo, Neiss took it upon himself to go to Washington and to seek ways of changing what he felt were anachronistic and outdated regulations that were stymying not only his own efforts to build a company but doubtless those of many others.

Neiss and his partners Jason Best and Zak Cassady-Dorion are credited with having been a three-man band of reluctant lobbyists who shepherded the JOBS Act through the halls of Congress and the Senate to its signing at the White House. Their citizen voices represented the silent entrepreneurs and investors who wanted to raise capital for and invest in small companies; their focus at all times was the passing of Regulation Crowdfunding—Regulation CF.

Occupying the halls of power Neiss was traversing were the people he most wanted to influence and educate: the politicians and their staff. By the time it passed, the JOBS Act of 2012 had become a collection of capital formation bills that had been circulating in Congress for several months. Traditionally, bills are named after the politicians who sponsor them, but much of the work that goes into formulating these bills from inception to legislation to promulgation is done by staff, the unsung heroes of the political process.

In contrast to the advocates and real estate visionaries, who each had little-to-no awareness of others involved in the JOBS Act, or what their role might be, the staffers coming next in the book on both sides of the aisle and in the White House worked closely with each other to craft the Act. The next three chapters contain the stories of these influential leaders, who focused on the importance of capital formation to small businesses. Each approached their role in the Act from the context of their own experience and political orientation.

In Chap. 5, Senate Lead Staffer **Dina Ellis Rochkind**, who has been dubbed the person who "wrote the JOBS Act," was working for Senator Pat Toomey (R-Pennsylvania) and was at the sharp end of much of the lobbying for capital formation regulation. Rochkind was sympathetic to the plight of established companies that needed capital not through public markets, but by expanding their existing shareholder base. Her role was pivotal in the formation for the JOBS Act because without an increase in shareholder limits for small companies, none of the other sections of the Act would function. Rochkind was also instrumental in preparing the entirety of the Act in her capacity as lead staffer in the Senate.

On the other side of the aisle, so to speak, **Andy Green** worked for Senator Jeff Merkley (D-Oregon) and his story occupies Chap. 6, Investor Protections. Andy entered the picture at a time when the economy had tanked, small companies had been almost completely squeezed out of capital markets, banks were under strain, and the value of their collateral had all but evaporated. Green was supportive of reinvigorating the capital formation opportunities for companies at the smaller end of the scale, but with the proviso that they not come at the expense of investor protections. He was driven by an awareness that history has repeatedly shown us that the most vulnerable people in society, those who can least afford to lose money when things go wrong, are usually those most often left shouldering the burdens of the excesses of the wealthy. Green was instrumental in drafting Regulation CF and, together with his colleagues, can be credited with having given the name to "funding portals." Green's perspective is double barreled because, after the Act was passed, he went on to work on actually writing the rules at the SEC.

Over at the White House in Chap. 7, **Doug Rand** was guiding disparate but interested parties through the process of making law. Rand worked on President Obama's JOBS Act team and has been described by advocates he worked with as the player in a game of chess where they were merely the pieces being moved around and he was the mastermind behind everything. His work entailed researching the concept of "crowdfunding" and soliciting opinions of those who had an interest in this form of capital formation so their insights could be used to craft legislation. Once he located these experts and advocates, he assisted them in navigating the labyrinthine processes of the Washington political machine.

The book now moves on to visionary real estate industry participants who were among the first to see that the JOBS Act had the potential to change the real estate industry. Doubtless there are others who also saw the potential, but the difference between potential and actuality is action, and in the following chapters you'll find the stories of those who were among the earliest to connect the dots with new legislation, and who took action and created a new industry at the intersection of real estate and tech.

Each real estate leader seeded their own ideas and vision completely independently of each other. None were inspired by anyone else to begin; each followed their own line of original thought. However, being competitive in nature, learning of others working along similar lines may have motivated each of them to persevere. Several conceived of the need for crowdfunded capital formation in real estate before the JOBS Act was even contemplated; it was clearly a need in real estate for which demand had been building for some time.

Chapter 8 introduces the first of the real estate entrepreneurs. It covers one of the earliest advocates for real estate crowdfunding in concept, if not in name, **Harold Hofer**, Rich Uncles. Long before the JOBS Act was passed Hofer had been thinking about how to bring the benefits of real estate investing that he had enjoyed throughout his career to everyone else. He understood that to encourage investment in real estate for everyone, minimum investment hurdles would have to be reduced. Starting in 2006, his first attempt at crowdfunding was stymied by the onset of the Great Recession that kicked in shortly after he started.

When the impact of the JOBS Act made it clear that lower minimum investments would become commonplace for real estate capital formation, Hofer's interest in reviving his idea was awakened. He dusted off his pre-JOBS Act investment minimum of $2500, reintroduced it to benefit from the momentum that the Act brought, and then reduced it further to $500. Once he started to build some momentum, riding the wave the Act had created, Hofer's long-term strategy evolved to focus on the millennial generation. To do this, his company started offering shares in their REIT (real estate investment trust) with a minimum $5 investment.

It is said that the millennial generation will likely never be able to build as much wealth as their baby boomer parents' generation, but they will inherit the wealth of their parents. As baby boomers start to shake off their mortal coils, millennials will capture all that wealth and be anxious to invest it somewhere, preferably via their smartphones. Rich Uncles has tapped into this market because they are looking multigenerationally. Notably, Harold Hofer and his partner Ray Wirta saw and explored this opportunity long before the JOBS Act was even contemplated.

Also pioneering the idea that raising capital from everyday investors was imperative in the evolution of the real estate industry way before the JOBS Act was contemplated even in its earliest stages was **Ben Miller**, co-founder and CEO of Fundrise, whose story is told in Chap. 9. During the depths of the Great Recession of 2008 Miller saw a disconnect between the ultraconservative institutional capital view of investment opportunity in real estate and the hunger regular people had to make their communities better by investing directly in them. Creating the first real estate crowdfund platform before the JOBS Act had passed, Miller found a way for the general public to access his deals by creatively applying existing regulations. Based in Washington DC, Miller realized the process he had formulated worked, but it was cumbersome, time-consuming, and expensive. When the JOBS Act regulations became law, Miller's big vision to provide America's "everyman" access to real estate investing became a reality.

In Chap. 10, the story finds **Nav Athwal** of RealtyShares in California practicing law, investing in real estate, and discovering that there were more investment opportunities than his access to capital permitted him to pursue. He sought ways to fill his equity funnel. Athwal recognized there was an opportunity to introduce tech to the real estate industry and to connect investors with deals, but he quickly discovered that securities laws prohibited the intersection. The JOBS Act was passed after he was already working on building tech solutions to create an online marketplace for investors to meet sponsors, while continuing to look for legal solutions to the quandary that what he wanted to do was prohibited. Athwal's vision was to build a platform where anyone, anywhere, could invest in real estate. Much of his early work was in putting together the tech infrastructure that would allow this to happen. Early regulatory changes in the promulgation process allowed him to test his thesis by putting deals up online and to solicit investors. His first deals paved the way for him to raise some of the earliest venture capital to enter the sector and to start building both his sponsor and investor networks with a proven concept.

Enter Investor **Ian Ippolito** in Chap. 11. A serial tech startup entrepreneur, Ippolito retired in 2013 after successfully selling his latest company a year after the JOBS Act passed, but before any of the regulations were promulgated. Needing to find prudent investments for the proceeds of his exit, he found himself dissatisfied with traditional financial advice pointing him solely to stocks and bonds, so sought alternative investments to fill out his portfolio. Ippolito discovered real estate crowdfunding and took it upon himself to engage in detailed research, which he started sharing freely with anyone who had an interest, adding to the ecosystem of the industry through distributing market intelligence. Though certainly an accredited investor, Ippolito's story is one not unfamiliar to any member of the crowd; those folk looking to invest in real estate and having to tackle the uncertainties of navigating the waters of a new industry.

Realty Mogul **Jilliene Helman**, whose tale is told in Chap. 12, saw the JOBS Act as the opening of a door to a marketing opportunity. For her, it was an obvious opening; one that had always been there, but one she'd never pursued because traditional fund-raising thinking and methodology dominated the industry. For Helman it wasn't because the law changed that she saw opportunity; existing law worked just fine for what she envisioned the future would look like. Rather, the law changed so visibly and generated such broad media coverage and press that made her understand that a tidal wave of change was upon the industry and it was one she could ride. Helman wanted to create a private network so investors could create syndications for real estate projects. She knew private networks were permitted prior to the JOBS Act, but without publicity around them, they had never before gained much credibility among accredited investors. When the Act passed, Helman recognized how the enormous publicity generated would create interest in real estate investment opportunities and investing syndications, so she rode this wave of visibility to build a business.

Picking himself up in Chap. 13 from the depths of collapse during the Great Recession and taking a path through the Amazonian rain forests comes the story of **Jason Fritton**, founder of Patch of Land. Fritton is an ambitious, self-motivated, highly driven serial entrepreneur. He does not accept defeat, no matter the circumstances. Having suffered some unimaginable setbacks, Fritton set about finding a way to build a future for himself by systematically looking at options for starting a new business. He had lost his home and business during the Great Recession and, completely independent of any experience in real estate, saw opportunity to do good for society by financing fix-and-flip investors. Fritton was committed to mending the flaws in finance, of which he, himself, had fallen victim. He was unaware (1) of the limitations the law placed on his idea, (2) that the laws were in the process of being amended, or (3) that others were thinking in the same way he was. His idea for a crowdfunded real estate site was his own original thought, born solely out of this creative entrepreneurial mind and a passion to do good and to help others.

The final chapter before drawing conclusions and, gasp, predicting where the industry is headed is the inspiring tale of **Eve Picker**, founder of one of the first Regulation CF platforms, Small Change. Coming from an architecture background and having developed real estate for a long time in challenging inner-city areas, Picker was accustomed to patching together financing for her tough projects from whatever sources were available. As her modus operandi was to find properties that revitalized neighborhoods, she often found that the economics of her deals were difficult to quantify and consequently challenging to finance. When government support of community development projects was curtailed, Picker's development activities were put on hold. Yet, she continued to yearn to improve underserved areas of Pittsburgh, her hometown.

Having been introduced by a friend to the new legislation the JOBS Act enacted, Picker was fascinated by the potential that real estate investment could be for everyone. She realized that in this was laid the opportunity for people to become truly vested in their own neighborhoods. She decided to explore opportunities and, being driven by the greater good, decided to set up a funding portal under Regulation CF to provide an avenue for developers and investors to meet, rather than using the Act to raise capital for her own projects. Picker did not choose the easiest route for bringing real estate investment opportunities to ordinary Americans and to local developers. Setting up and operating a funding portal, she discovered, was one of the hardest things she had ever endeavored to do. Eve Picker is the last leader covered in this book, bringing as she does the benefits of true crowd investment to a neighborhood near you.

Together, this cadre of pioneers became the *Leaders of the Crowd*.

2

Inception: David Weild IV

David Weild IV is a scientist by training. He started his career as an academic biologist who really didn't like biology but who liked genetics, fulfilling most of his undergraduate requirements with graduate course work in molecular genetics. He left graduate programs, ultimately finding himself on Wall Street, and was fascinated when watching Genentech go public (1980): seeing the stock open at $35 per share and cresting within an hour at more than $88.

It was one of the largest stock run-ups ever and Weild was bitten by the bug of capital formation. He was smitten with the thought that capital could result in great contributions and world progress. His father, a Yale Law School graduate and intellectual properties attorney, and he used to have great debates at the dinner table about whether or not genetic engineering was going to be patentable because genetics are naturally occurring and as such typically are not patentable. Weild always believed that from a public policy standpoint, someone would have to figure out a way to make it patentable or risk a missed opportunity for the investment required to forward progress in healthcare. These were formative discussions for Weild, who has always been driven to do good for his community and his country. If barriers are premised solely on traditional and not logical thinking, and were contrary to society's best interest, Weild's inclination has always been to find ways to break them down.

The experience of watching Genentech, essentially a startup, explode onto the public markets in the manner in which it did was the beginning of a fascination with small growth companies for Weild. He attended the *New York University Stern School of Business*, graduated, and took a position on Wall Street, working in the equity capital markets group at Prudential Securities. There he had a range of positions and was lucky enough to be promoted relatively quickly. Promotions led to increased responsibility.

Having a wide variety of responsibilities, mostly in corporate finance, his position evolved to become one where his primary role was to take companies public. Small then, but big today—*Nvidia*, for example, which is the three-dimensional chip company founded by Jen-Hsun Huang. He was instrumental in the early days of *Celgene*, which has had a market cap in excess of $100 billion in market value. When Weild was working on it, it was only a $100 million company trying to take a very controversial drug (thalidomide) back into the market. Thalidomide had been banned because it caused birth defects, but new research suggested some tremendous benefit potential. Weild also raised the very first assets from the public for Blackrock. Today, Blackrock is the largest asset manager in the world with over $1 trillion under management.

By the time Weild was aware of the falloff in the number of initial public offerings (IPOs) on US markets, which he ultimately was to track the cause to the reduction in tick size and electronic market structure, he had already priced over a thousand public equity offerings and had become recognized as a foremost innovator in the arena. There's a variety of corporate finance techniques that are applied in public equities markets and many started with an innovation that Weild introduced back in the 1990s. One idea was to use shelf-registrations to stealth-market publicly traded companies and shield them from short sellers and market risk, thus delivering better price execution and lower cost of capital to corporate issuers. Being recognized for his successes in capital markets, Weild found himself progressively getting kicked upstairs. The last job he had at Prudential was as president of PrudentialFinancial.com, where he ran their global Internet businesses.

This role very much connected Weild to the Internet and some of the things that were going on with market structure. This along with Weild's experience with corporate issuers drew the attention of his mentor, Chairman and CEO of Prudential Securities at the time, Hardwick ("Wick") Simmons. Simmons had worked with some notables over the course of his career, including Arthur Levitt—who later became the longest serving Chair in the history of the SEC—and Sanford "Sandy" Weill—who ran Citibank and who remains a legend in the industry for having persuaded Congress to repeal the Glass Steagall Act, which allowed him to create the first financial supermarket since the Great Depression and had led to the separation of JP Morgan from Morgan Stanley. Weill would later regret his lobbying because it contributed to "too big to fail" institutions, whose near-collapse led in part to the Great Recession of 2008–2009. When Simmons went over as chairman and CEO of Nasdaq, Weild followed him over to be vice chairman and executive vice president in charge of all the listed companies, globally.

It was that experience, combined with his history of having taken companies public, that allowed him to gain insight into the regulatory side of business and how the SEC's changes to rules and market structure were impacting market making, equity research, distribution, and ultimately the entire ecosystem that was required to support companies that were trying to access public markets. Weild was, in short, one of the rare people that had actually priced hundreds of IPOs and who sat in a quasi-regulatory position. Now he was interacting with those who were implementing and reporting on market structure changes. This privileged oversight helped him to connect the dots between Congressional and SEC rulemaking and the precipitous falloff in IPO activity.

Other Nasdaq executives expressed their concern over Weild for unabashedly saying that Nasdaq had created an "incredible delisting machine" in the wake of the dot com bubble; there was not enough economic incentive for people to make markets in support of microcap stocks, he said. Weild saw an environment hostile to smaller cap companies that had been opened up to predatory short selling. This often illegal short selling was systematically causing large numbers of companies to be delisted.

To temporarily correct this problem Weild worked with the SEC who, to their credit, were very receptive to implementing a moratorium on the rule that required the delisting from Nasdaq of any company whose stock price breaks a dollar per share for some period of time. By creating breathing room for at-risk-of-delisting public companies, companies would be saved and jobs would be saved. The "bubble rubble" in the wake of the dotcom boom's bust after the Internet's "irrational exuberance"—in the words of Alan Greenspan—would have less bite.

During that period of collapse it was very easy for predatory short sellers to push stocks down below a dollar a share, forcing them to delist. The result—they'd pretty much go to zero—after which the predatory short sellers would cover their positions and make a killing.

This offended Weild's notion of fair play. At the time, companies were under a great deal of pressure, politically and socially, to keep people employed. The SEC approved of Weild's idea and allowed the Nasdaq to put a moratorium in place on those delistings, helping many companies. This experience focused Weild's attention on how market structure could be abused to the detriment of the employers and, particularly, those smaller companies that are most in need of access to public markets.

The Collapse of Small Cap Liquidity

There was another change to small cap access to public capital that was to profoundly influence Weild's life, and to put him on a path that would ultimately lead to the JOBS Act. In the late 1990s, market regulations shifted in a way that effectively cut small companies out of the capital markets by removing the incentives brokers needed to trade small company shares. Historically, brokers would make a commission on the margin between the buy and the sell price of a stock. The relative importance of commission-based trading is different for small and large cap stocks. When the well-intentioned SEC reformed commission structures, Weild witnessed a disproportionately negative impact on small cap companies.

For example: a large cap, highly liquid stock has sellers for 500,000 shares. There are buyers for these shares and the market finds equilibrium. There is no real need for dealers to assist the transaction because as long as buyers and sellers exist on both sides of the market and can find each other (i.e., online), they will trade. In fact, to force the market to pay commissions in highly efficient (innately liquid) market scenarios such as this creates economic friction by adding an unnecessary layer of complexity and cost.

In 1997 and 1998, in an effort to eliminate this "tax" on investors, SEC Chairman Arthur Levitt forced Nasdaq market makers to abandon their practice of 25 cent ($0.25) increment pricing of securities and collapsed the margin, the "tick" size, to just a little more than 3 cents ($0.03125) upon which a broker could make a commission intermediating a trade, effectively removing the economic incentive for the broker to intercede. By 2001, the minimum tick size was further degraded to 1 cent ($0.01).

Weild saw this lead to one of the great unintended consequences of well-intended market structure changes. Levitt thought that the SEC was going to save investors' money and protect consumers by reducing the tick size so that online trading could become more efficient—but what they also did was put more pressure on the economy by dropping the bottom out of the small cap stock market. The stock brokers who supported stocks through "storytelling" faced financial ruin and had to quickly abandon the stock broking business and pursue careers as asset gatherers, who would now recommend funds in place of stocks.

Take, for example, the small cap company. When a small cap company that normally trades only 20,000 shares has sellers for 500,000, somebody has to be able to make money to go out and find 500,000 shares worth of buyers to offset that seller. When you get into stocks which don't have lots of buyers and sellers, you've got to have an economic model to pay for the research analysts and salespeople to develop an investment and price thesis and call investors. These are the salespeople who call customers to create buyers to offset sellers and alleviate what can be disastrous pressure on small cap stock prices. These folk need to be incentivized. Their compensation used to come from incentives that were premised on higher tick sizes, trading spreads and commissions.

When tick sizes, trading spreads, and commissions collapsed, the margin that a broker could make on a transaction was effectively eliminated. Brokers would phone the prospect with the story of the stock, explaining company background, benefits of the stock, and so on. When that educational storytelling process dried up, smaller cap companies found themselves in a wasteland of exposure, unseen by the investing public.

Indeed, one of the great misconceptions of the markets in the Internet age is that there is plenty of information and plenty of access to information that is going to drive liquidity for small cap company stocks. In fact, information is only the precursor to the hard work required to analyze a company and develop a view on business fundamentals and stock price. It is certainly true that when you're dealing with symmetrical order book stocks, there are economies of scale for large investors to do the research—as a result, most quality research analysts flee Wall Street to find jobs with the "buy side" (e.g., hedge funds, mutual funds). Where there are thousands of buyers and sellers at any point in time, there's plenty of analysis and liquidity available, but this is only true of large cap stocks. It works for Intel, it works for Microsoft, it works for Exxon Mobile, but it doesn't work for the vast majority of small companies that need to access public markets—the very companies that drive innovation and growth and create jobs for the US economy.

Policymakers failed to understand that the level of innate liquidity and visibility for large cap stocks is orders of magnitude higher than that of microcap stocks. The creation of one-size-fits-all electronic markets that were optimized for large cap trading was doomed from the outset to fail microcap markets that really must depend on research and sales. Small and microcap stocks require a research analyst to support investors and sales professionals. It's the salesman who has a trusted customer relationship that can talk to an investor-client and to create demand at that particular point in time when the stock becomes available for sale in the marketplace. Electronic markets that disintermediate professionals cannot provide the economic model needed to cover this essential function.

It's really a question of large cap stocks having critical mass orders always at the ready, while small cap stocks do not. Most people still need somebody that they trust to get on the phone with them and tell them a story about some unknown but potentially exciting stock. People need an easy way to understand why a company is worth the investment. Otherwise, investors gravitate toward large cap companies with big brands that they know, and institutional investors focus their internal research muscle on large cap stocks that are innately liquid, thereby allowing them to spread the cost of their investment in research across large stock positions and multiple portfolios. Small cap stock support and marketing is a much more labor-intensive business than professionals, regulators, or even Congress ever believed.

When electronic markets were introduced and tick sizes were cut, trading spreads collapsed and commissions were all but eliminated. Investors started to trade in the newly emerging online marketplaces. Small cap companies lost their support. The institutional and sales infrastructure required to broadly distribute and support IPOs began to erode and the incentive to go public, for all but the largest companies (and those that had no alternative), was removed. The onerous costs of going public, combined with the lack of distribution and aftermarket support, dissuaded most small cap companies from seeking public capital. This caused the decline in the number of IPOs. Weild saw the stark impact firsthand and was the first to document it. In the wake of the dotcom bubble, the number of IPOs went from about 540 IPOs a year to about 120; the percentage of small IPOs dropped from 80 percent of all IPOs to only 20 percent and never recovered. Indeed, regulators had raised the bar so high on going public that companies and their investment bankers were now avoiding US public markets.

The loss of the small IPO had a depressive effect on the economy. Historically, an active IPO market provided capital to companies—capital that was then invested. Much of that investment activity resulted in people getting hired. Those new employees then spent money in the economy, which, in turn, created more jobs. This so-called multiplier effect was thrown into reverse with the government-induced collapse of the IPO market. This, in turn, helped slow down the economy and contributed to unemployment. Weild explains that it is no coincidence that the reduction in IPOs and the increase in delistings of small cap companies coincided with the economic difficulties that were experienced, leading up to and including the financial crisis of 2008. The US government shot itself in its economic foot.

Moreover, in the run-up to the 2008 crash and Great Recession, while there was a real estate boom going on, the United States did not enjoy the job creation that had been experienced in other economic cycles. Weild believes that these "missing jobs" were due to the collapse in IPO activity and support for small public companies, which combined he calls a "key component in the reinvention engine of the US economy" and why President Jiang Zemin of China once called Nasdaq "the crown jewel of the US economy."

Simply stated, if the bar is raised on going public, then there will be less capital available for small companies and startups. This, in turn, will put a damper on job growth. Weild actually predicted that the number of startups would decline in the United States with the loss of the IPO market and indeed it has. In 2016, the United States reached a 40-year low in startup activity.

Weild has had this conversation with Mike Piwowar, a commissioner at the SEC and a PhD economist who Weild first met when Piwowar worked for Senator Richard Shelby. Their debate centered around whether the collapse in economic incentives to Wall Street was the "cause and effect" of the IPO decline or whether it was "correlation." Weild had run the IPO business at one of the major Wall Street investment banks and, in 1999, he ran strategic planning for their investment banking, equity research institutional sales, and institutional trading groups.

At that time, it was very clear that one of the 1997 "Big Bang" changes called the "Order Handling Rules," was followed by the electronic stock market. This further disintermediated the broker. Then came a rule called the Alternative Trading System (Regulation ATS), in 1998, that was a one-two punch. The rule stated that when a customer's orders were placed, the orders have to be reflected into the market through an electronic bulletin board. To facilitate this, regulators took Nasdaq-quoted spreads from a quarter-point overnight down to an electronic spread, for the most part, of a 32nd, which is 3.125 cents. The so-called tick size.

This is what killed the broker function. The spread upon which a broker could be paid went from 25 basis points, to just over 3 basis points, as previously mentioned. For a broker, that meant that they had to take a commission of some sort based on the difference between the buy and the ask spread of a share, so if that spread went down to so small an increment, the room for a commission was substantially reduced. Then, to Weild's consternation, in 2001 Arthur Levitt and the SEC went ahead and decimalized the market, taking the tick size down to a penny—to just 1 basis point—and in so doing the broker lost literally 96 percent of the economic incentive to make markets in microcap stocks.

This meant that in the four-year period from 1997 to 2001 liquidity for small cap companies had completely collapsed because the incentive to promote their stocks, post going public, had been eviscerated.

Weild saw in this the perfect cause and effect. The effect was to take traders out of small cap stocks. Analysts migrated exclusively into large cap stocks and it became crystal clear the bottom was being dropped out of the small cap market. For Weild this was not an intellectual exercise and riled his sense of social justice. He watched it impacting people's lives and the rationalization for it was that it was saving consumers' money was counterintuitive for Weild. Although it was probably true in terms of large cap stocks, Weild was witnessing the gutting of the most important IPO market that the world had ever seen and the consequent elimination of capital formation where the country most needed it—at the small cap end of the market.

America had had an IPO market that birthed entirely new industries, driving US competitiveness. President Jiang Jiemin's view that Nasdaq was the crown jewel of the US economy was because of the innovation the system spawned from smaller cap startups being capitalized by the public markets and Weild was watching it being undone.

Though well-intentioned, the result of this intervention in a system that was working very well was that fewer small companies were being created particularly in the Heartland. Weild accepts that there were, and are, ecosystems to replace the old public market ecosystem, but he notes that it tends to be very geographically constrained. Places like Silicon Valley are doing just fine, but even they have morphed. Where before they would do A, B, and C rounds from a venture capital standpoint, then do an IPO for an exit, today they're doing the D, E, F, G, H, I, J, K on to a Z round. And only then might they take the company public. More and more large institutional funds were set up to pour massive amounts of capital into these companies to fill the gap left by the lack of public capital.

Weild sees this as creating a have and have-not world. It's harder to get things bootstrapped and the Heartland is particularly badly hit because there are certain geographies that are highly funded by the venture capital community, like New York, San Francisco, and Boston. These areas are probably going to do better than many other cities and many other regions.

This disparity animated Weild, who did not believe that, as a country, this was where we wanted to be. This enormous gap was simply inequitable and unjust. He didn't see anyone doing two or three or four rounds of financing from friends and family and local investors and then accessing public markets. It drove wholesale rethinking of the financing strategy of what's an interesting idea and it caused the venture capital industry to invest differently than they would if they had an IPO market that allowed them to get $25–30 million IPOs done the way they had in the past.

Weild cites the Intel IPO all the way back in 1971 as a classic example of something great in America, something lost when the IPO market became so inaccessible. Intel was only an $8-million IPO. Even in today's terms if you tripled the size, it would still only be a $24-million IPO. This was a company that wasn't profitable on an operating basis when it went public, missing delivery on its first product, and seeing the stock traded down 70 percent. But the broker community was earning big fat commissions at the time and they turned the ship around by getting the stock seen. At that time, salesmen were able to get on the phone and earn a living; they had a story to tell and they sold it to people and the rest is history.

You could not do an Intel IPO in today's markets and the tragedy of that is what drove Weild to want to change the dynamic by bringing liquidity back where it needed to be—into the hands of the entrepreneurs struggling to finance their small companies' growth.

Thought Leadership

To bring the change Weild wanted, he co-wrote and published a series of papers to raise awareness. The first group of these thought leadership papers was published through the accounting firm, Grant Thornton. One of them was called "The Trouble with Small Tick Sizes," and another was entitled "Why Are IPOs in the ICU?" They formed the core arguments behind a series of recommendations made for public and private markets to bring liquidity back, especially to small companies. One of Weild's key recommendations was the repeal of the prohibition against general solicitation which was to directly lead to a form of crowdfunding called 506(c). 506(c) is an exemption from public securities registration under Regulation D of the 1933 Securities Act.

Weild had accepted that IPOs had become an expensive and inefficient way for small cap companies to raise capital. Even if they did go public, the market for their shares had collapsed. Weild considered that, if public markets were inaccessible, perhaps private markets might provide capital resources sorely needed by small companies.

Weild figured that by bringing accredited investors into private placements to replace the public option, one could create the liquidity that was needed. To do this effectively, he reasoned, companies would have to be allowed to market broadly. However, the way that the private placement rules worked at that point was that, while it was legal to raise money from private sources, it was done under an exemption from public registration known as Regulation D, 506(b). The problem with this, Weild knew, was that to use this exemption, you needed to have a reasonable belief that the person or entity one approached was accredited; meaning one could not generally advertise a private placement lest someone who saw the advertisement was not accredited.

To resolve this quandary, Weild asked a pretty simple question: *Why do we care who we tell the story to?* Wouldn't it be a great idea if Mark Zuckerberg, before Facebook went public, could get on TV without fear of retaliation and talk about his business? The public, obviously, would be ravenously interested in what Mark Zuckerberg would have had to say before Facebook went public. Yet he couldn't do that without conditioning the market and creating a great delay to an IPO and slamming the window on his ability to raise private placement capital. The same should just as easily apply to small cap companies and startups, Weild concluded.

As a rule, the folk at the SEC agreed that the current restrictions didn't make a lot of sense; that it would be beneficial to come up with an alternative to allow capital raisers to more broadly solicit accredited investors. Only after soliciting would they be obligated to make sure that the investor that came into this private placement was, in fact, accredited.

What actually emerged as a result of Weild's proposal was workable, with some nuances. The old form of private placements asked an investor to self-proclaim as an accredited investor and check a series of boxes. In what emerged from the JOBS Act, the new form typically required having to get a third party to verify accreditation. That might be an investor's registered investment advisor or Certified Public Accountant (CPA) or attorney or broker dealer. This adjustment gave birth to 506(c)—one of most important contributions to crowdfunding because it allows for general solicitation or, in other words, allows for advertising online.

Weild had seeded the digital commerce equivalent of the old school salesman, the pre-1997 broker. Being allowed to advertise meant that a company owner, the sponsor, could now tell their own story to prospects and be permitted to solicit investment directly. The broker is gone, but the storytelling has returned.

The other form of crowdfunding which was oriented to the general public, accredited and non-accredited alike, was a piece of legislation that Weild had proposed to Congress, and that had been picked up originally through Representative Patrick McHenry. This was rolled up into the JOBS Act with the epithet Regulation CF.

When it started out with the first version in the House and its cap of $5 million, a lot of people became concerned that it was going to be public investors investing in it. Even though the proposal was that these investors were limited to $5000 in capital per deal, it got whittled down and the version that the House sent to the Senate had a $2 million cap. And, ultimately, it was cut to $1 million by the Senate.

As a result of the $1-million cap, and even though any investor from the public could be brought into a deal, it ended up really not as meaningful as Weild, or others, intended it to be.

Transformational Impact

Overall, Weild thinks that general solicitation for private placements, the freedom to advertise, is the most impactful component of the JOBS Act. It spawned a cottage industry of online marketplaces that are aggregating accredited investors and financing small companies—the very place where innovation and job formation occur. Weild likes to reference Professor Enrico Moretti at the University of California at Berkeley. Moretti wrote a book called *The New Geography of Jobs* and in it he says that for every technology job that's created, there are five service sector jobs that are created. There's a multiplier effect and Weild sees that as being particularly true in small companies in general. If you can raise capital you employ people, those people spend money in the economy. If you can elevate the level of activity you're going to see a greater velocity of money and that's going to be very stimulating.

Congressional Testimony

Weild testified, in Congress, his support of the JOBS Act because he and his colleagues were considered the intellectual capital that framed the problem. He had identified the small IPO and defined it as a sub-$50-million IPO that had actually fallen off a cliff in 1997–1998—two years before decimalization and three years before Sarbanes-Oxley, which were popularly considered to be the culprits. Weild demonstrated to Congress that the falloff in public market liquidity for small cap companies had happened during the height of the dot-com bubble when nobody was looking. There was this sort of pathology that had been unleashed on the low end of the market. Weild described the small tick sizes and electronic markets as being like a "flesh-eating bacteria that were eating at the bottom of the market," eating their way up through the ecosystem. The concept was a revelation for Congress.

He also documented the number of listed companies over time and showed that the United States not only had seen a precipitous decline—dropping from 9000 publicly listed companies down to 5000—but that it was also clear that not enough IPOs were being done to replace what was being taken out of the markets.

Weild described to Congress that they were presiding over rapidly shrinking public markets while foreign markets were doing better than America. European markets were doing better. The Chinese were crushing it and they were up 91 percent, while markets in the States were down by over 40 percent.

Several slides Weild used in his testimony were picked up in the House Financial Services Committee and the Subcommittee on Capital Markets and displayed to the members of Congress. To the consternation of one congressmen who questioned Weild, one comparative chart looking at the different countries had China at the top and the United States at the bottom. "Top or bottom," Weild asked. "Which one would you prefer to be?"

The point he made drew everybody's attention.

Leaving a Legacy

At the end of the day, what drives Weild is his passion about this country. He cares about the future of the nation's children and about leaving a legacy for the next generation. He believes that the tool kit we need goes beyond survival; it's the ability to thrive. And that success comes through innovation that drives economic growth.

Sound economic infrastructure through strong capital markets is absolutely critical to where we go and how we do as a nation. Unfortunately, it's a fairly complicated subject for most people. It's not intuitive and we still have a heck of a lot of work to do. Today Weild runs a company, an investment bank, called Weild and Co. There they aggregate investment banking human capital required to do due diligence. They kick the tires on deals and package deals to help corporations access capital markets because Weild continues to believe that the market still needs people to tell stories.

JOBS Act

Though it's not perfect, the JOBS Act has helped with capital formation in America. Weild thought it would be slow to take hold; changes promulgated by the SEC generally take longer than expected before the market adopts new rules. The securities bar is very risk averse and, generally, advisors don't want their clients being first. It's like penguins at the edge of an ice floe—huddling and waiting for the first one to jump. If the first doesn't get swallowed by a shark, then the rest of them will take the plunge.

There were some early delays, not just in the pace at which the rules were promulgated, but in the way Congress wrote the legislation. The only meaningful part of the JOBS Act that went into effect right away was Title I, which is the new designation of emerging growth company. Titles II, III, and IV, which included crowdfunding, 506(c), and Regulation A+, which Weild refers to as "IPO Light," respectively, all required the SEC to write rules before they could be enacted and, hence, this led to the early delays.

Plus, at the time, the SEC was torn in their priorities surrounding rulemaking for the JOBS Act. They were also working on Dodd Frank, which was massive. Weild remarks in disbelief that, apparently, the Federal Register includes 25 million words on rulemaking in Dodd Frank. It's hardly surprising, he observes, that it was such a monumental task for the SEC and tough for them to work simultaneously on the JOBS Act.

Weild is not a fan of Dodd Frank; he'd prefer to see it repealed. He likes the idea of going back to Glass Steagall, which he sees as having been a simple and elegant solution. Everybody understood the separation between the risk and the nonrisk businesses. In Weild's mind, if you're too big to fail, you're just too big. "Why," he asks, "are we messing around with these behemoth financial institutions when we don't need to? Glass Steagall worked very well. It was passed all the way back in 1933 in the wake of the crash of 1927 and in the midst of the Great Depression when the combination of risk (investment banking) and non-risk businesses (lending) led to losses that in turn nearly collapsed the banks when depositors tried to get their money out."

Weild sees that we did pretty much the same thing in the credit crisis of 2008–2009, during a period when Treasury notes were trading above par. People were willing to pay the US government to hold their money and to lose money on that proposition because, at least, they were guaranteed to get that money back. Hank Paulson, then Secretary of the Treasury, had the wisdom to wrap the full faith in and credit of the US Treasury around the banking system. Without that we would have been, without any question, plunged into another Great Depression.

JOBS Act Impact on Real Estate Never Considered

Weild, and everyone else, was focused on the impact on operating companies while working on the JOBS Act. Real estate wasn't on the top of anyone's list. In fact, Weild says, it didn't figure in at all when the JOBS Act was being debated, written, and passed.

Weild is delighted to learn that real estate is one of those happy outcomes of the JOBS Act: a positive unintended consequence. In hindsight it makes sense to him. There's a lot more investment appetite with retail accredited investors for yield-oriented instruments, like real estate, and there always has been. Weild raised public money for Larry Fink and BlackRock—now the largest financial institution in the world—and for a great many, very large, closed-end funds, but it was always the yield-oriented closed-end funds that found the greatest retail audience.

What Weild likes especially about the impact on real estate is born out of his drive to do good for society on a broader, local level. When you're dealing with smaller amounts of capital there's an argument to be made that you are potentially bringing capital into smaller real estate properties and into smaller jurisdictions. There is a lot of large-scale institutional grade capital, for instance, in real estate. The public real estate investment trust market, for example, focused on very large properties. Access to capital and, more broadly, to real estate and to more jurisdictions is probably helpful to long-term economic growth.

Weild has variously been called a "Wall Street legend," a "visionary," an "oracle," even "The Shaman," and, most frequently, "the Father of the JOBS Act." Whichever epithet is used, it is certain that his insights into the causes of the decline of the small cap market in America, and the solutions he advocated, seeded the Act before it was a twinkle in anyone else's eye.

3

The Letter: Jenny Kassan

Jenny Kassan has always been an activist who wanted to make the world a better place. She decided to study law and graduated from Yale Law School because, although she was not quite sure what she was going to do with a law degree, she thought being a lawyer would help her achieve her goal. Between college and law school, she looked around for something to do that would be interesting and took a position in Washington DC at the Institute for Policy Studies where she was paired with a fellow called Michael Shuman.

Michael had always been interested in the importance of localism and believed that all good things that happen in the world start from the grassroots and trickle up. Jenny had never really thought about things that way, having become accustomed to focusing more on national and international policy. Michael's perspective that real change gets made at the local level was inspirational for Jenny.

With this newfound, deep sense of "local," Jenny started looking at why very few small businesses have much access to capital. She saw that almost all invested capital in America goes through Wall Street and into giant public companies. The huge mismatch of capital was troubling given half of the US economy is produced by small businesses. She wondered why nearly 100 percent of capital is invested in only 50 percent of the economy.

After law school, Jenny moved to Oakland and started working at a nonprofit doing community development. One of her jobs there was to work with small businesses in low-income communities. This got her even more passionate about the extremely uneven playing field of small business versus giant public companies.

Jenny left the nonprofit after Shuman introduced her to a securities lawyer named John Katovich. Katovich had been the chief counsel at *The Pacific Stock Exchange* and was starting a small law firm to help businesses raise money.

This was Jenny's first exposure to the law governing business finance, also known as securities law. She joined the law firm and worked really hard to learn and understand securities law, enjoying the process very much. With no preconceived ideas at the onset, she discovered later that a lot of lawyers have a very incomplete understanding of securities law because they tend to use a cookie cutter approach for all of their clients and don't take the time to understand what all the different options are.

Through Katovich, Jenny learned there was this thing called a "direct public offering," an instrument that had been used previously to raise capital. Ben and Jerry's, for example, had done a direct public offering of securities in Vermont in 1984 and, although it never became really common, other companies had also used that type of offering.

Jenny learned that although there was a legal way to do a public offering of securities, it was still pretty onerous because you had to register state by state. To assist clients with this process, Jenny decided to specialize in this type of offering and started spreading the gospel that it was possible to raise investment capital by "crowdfunding," and she became recognized as an expert in guiding clients through the various hurdles they would face.

Together with her partner, Jenny looked for clients who wanted to do public offerings and, in 2006, they found their first client who was based in New

York. Jenny did all the work to get them through the regulatory process that would allow them to raise money from investors in New York, Connecticut, and New Jersey, but the client ended up deciding not to go forward with it. Another client came along who did it just in California, and little by little, Jenny's practice started and her client base began to grow.

The process was that she identified an applicable federal exemption from the requirement to do a full federal registration of the offering, which allowed her clients to avoid the extremely onerous and expensive federal registration process. Typically, her clients used either the intrastate exemption, provided they were only offering securities within that one state, or Rule 504, which at that time allowed clients to raise up to $1 million, and they could do a public offering in more than one state.

After identifying the appropriate federal exemption, Jenny would complete the applicable state registrations. This process involved completing a prospectus and providing a bunch of information to the state securities regulators, who would eventually give the go ahead—but not before putting Jenny and her clients through the wringer for a few months, asking a lot of questions and making them add things to their prospectus. Each state was different. So in some states, like in Colorado, it might only take a few weeks for the process, whereas in others, like in California, it could take as long as five months.

Jenny and her partner had one client who registered in 16 different states, but most limited the registration to one or two. It was a pain because every state was different. There was a form called the Small Company Offering Registration (SCOR) form that could be used in multiple states, but in practice, each state's requirements were quite different.

One of her more famous clients was the People's Community Market in Oakland. Around 2011, they were trying to buy and renovate a building in order to operate a community supermarket. They tried to raise money in more traditional ways by going to a lot of pitch competitions and impact investor conferences, but hadn't had any success because, well, it was a grocery store and they couldn't pay the kind of returns these investors were looking for. Jenny helped them raise money using the process she had been working on, setting the minimum investment at $1000. They even had something where people who couldn't afford a thousand dollars could prepay for a gift card. They raised $1.7 million and brought on a lot of other partners and lenders and were able to put the financing together to get the deal off the ground. This was a major real estate development project in a low-income neighborhood tied to a business startup with a social mission.

Jenny really enjoyed helping her clients with these applications pre-JOBS Act, but at the same time, she was frustrated because it was a tough process and consequently, was costly for clients. While thinking through creative ideas for how to resolve these capital formation issues for clients, she was still talking to Michael Shuman who wrote an article for the *Federal Reserve Journal*.

The article made a simple proposal: wouldn't it be interesting if the SEC created an exemption where as long as no one invested more than $100, it was completely exempt from any regulatory requirements and there would be no need for any filings because the risk to each individual would be so low. Meanwhile, Paul Spinrad, who was with *Make Magazine*, reached out to Jenny because she had written another article on the topic. His encouragement motivated Jenny to persevere and "make it happen."

By this time, Jenny had co-founded a nonprofit called the Sustainable Economies Law Center (SELC) with Janelle Orsi, who is a creative attorney and outside-the-box thinker. Paul Spinrad proposed raising some funds to support the SELC by submitting a petition to the federal regulatory body in charge of securities, the SEC, to request an exemption like the one Michael Shuman had proposed.

To cover the cost of the project, Paul, Jenny, and Janelle raised $2000 on Indiegogo and the project proceeded at the SELC with two interns. They were directed to draft a letter to the SEC, laying out the argument for why there should be an exemption for sub-$100 investors.

Jenny signed the letter once it was completed and submitted it to the SEC, where, pursuant to SEC policy, it was put up on their website together with all the other submitted petitions. Once they submitted the letter, Paul, Jenny, and Janelle set about spreading the word. They told everyone they knew to go on the SEC website and post comments on the petition letter. It got some 150 positive comments, which was more than any petition had ever received before.

One thing led to another, including radio interviews and other coverage, and Woodie Neiss found out about it and ran with it, putting a ton of effort and time and energy toward advocating for this proposal. Meanwhile, the American Sustainable Business Council, which is a national advocacy organization, came on board to help advocate for the requested rule change.

Sadly, the SEC ignored the petition. However, the proposal began to get support from Congress and the White House and fairly quickly legislation was drafted.

Mary Schapiro, who at the time was the SEC Chair and who was dismissive of the whole idea, was openly challenged by Congressman Darrell Issa, who took her to task on her opposition to the proposal.

Doug Rand from Obama's office had seen the original letter Jenny wrote and had picked up the idea she floated. He liked the idea so he frequently talked to Jenny, asking her opinion as the process evolved and staying in touch.

He had Jenny on his list of people who were involved from the very beginning and recognized that she had initiated the process very early on.

Thanks to the efforts of lots of supporters the initiative took on a life of its own, so Jenny adjusted her role to allow other people who had really taken up the mantle to run with it. She focused on coordinating comments on the legislation and on the rulemaking process through the American Sustainable Business Council because she wanted to be sure that the ultimate result would be something practical and useful for small businesses and mom-and-pop shops.

The objective of Jenny's efforts was not to allow everyone to become a venture capitalist (VC), but rather it was all about supporting small businesses, regular businesses, and not necessarily only those in high tech with high growth potential. Not that those couldn't benefit as well, but Jenny believed that the whole point of what she was working on was to help the 99 percent of businesses that represent half of our economy; those made up of small businesses. Those were the ones most in need of easier access to capital, and Jenny wanted to be sure they continued to be represented as the process evolved.

The first version of the legislation was a simple bill proposed by Rep. Patrick McHenry. It was quite different from the original proposal—it capped investments at much more than $100 (the lesser of $10,000 or 10 percent of the investor's annual income). But Jenny and her team liked the proposed legislation because it was super short and simple. That version, called the Entrepreneur Access to Capital Act, passed the House of Representatives almost unanimously. Then, when it went to the Senate, the legislation was amended extensively with a lot of provisions added in the name of investor protection. For example, all investments would have to be made through an online intermediary that had to go through a regulatory process and become a member of the FINRA (Financial Industry Regulatory Authority), the nongovernmental regulatory body for the financial industry. The ultimate result was not as user-friendly as the original proposal but was still a major step in the right direction.

The main pushback Jenny came across while she was advocating for what was to become the JOBS Act, was that people thought it was too risky for investors because investors were perceived to be too unsophisticated. Opponents were concerned that vulnerable investors were going to lose all their money. There were lots of people saying that, which Jenny found ironic because as a pretty liberal person, there were a lot of people on the left, her usual allies, who were opposed to what she was trying to do. There was one organization that had to do with financial products for senior citizens, she recalls, who were especially worried about it.

There was an organization called Our Financial Security dot org. They were one of the main opponents, and Americans for Financial Reform were also staunch opponents. Jenny regretted their opposition because she thought they were well-intentioned, and she found it frustrating to be fighting against people she was normally totally in alignment with.

Jenny couldn't help but think that if people can go to the casino and lose all their money, why would there be restrictions on how they could invest? Ultimately, the authors of the Act tried to create a balance of making it fairly easy to use, but also putting some limits on it like creating an investor cap and maximizing the amount someone could invest relative to their overall wealth or income. The thinking was that if people can't invest any more than the lesser of 5 percent of their net worth or annual income, then in the worst-case scenario of losing everything they invested, they would still probably be OK.

Once the Act was passed, Jenny was surprised at how little understood the eventual bill seemed to be by the people involved. She and Michael Shuman attended the Rose Garden signing ceremony at which President Obama signed the JOBS Act into law. Afterward, they went to a celebration at a nearby bar. She recalls asking the other people at the celebration what they thought about the fact that intermediaries (also known as funding portals) were required to be FINRA members. Others in attendance were not aware of that provision of the law and it left Jenny feeling that she was the only person in the room who had really read the law.

Upon reflection, Jenny was driven by her sense of what she considered an injustice in the financial system; 99 percent of capital goes to support giant multinational corporations and, even then, not directly. She saw Wall Street as a huge casino with the odds tilted away from the little guy and she felt like America would be a better place, and its communities would be better off, if more small businesses could have access to affordable finance.

If community residents and regular folk could invest in and benefit from the success of local businesses, things would be fairer overall. Thomas Piketty's economics of inequality resonated for Jenny: If you don't have capital you stay poor because you can't invest in anything, and she thought everyone should have the opportunity to invest.

4

Advocate: Sherwood Neiss

Sherwood "Woodie" Neiss got his MBA in international finance from Thunderbird in Arizona, and from there he went to Wall Street, where he got a feel for how public companies raise capital in the public markets and how bureaucratically laden and costly the process is. He migrated to the retail side of things, which he didn't really care for very much, but there he came to realize he enjoyed finance technology software.

© The Author(s) 2018
A. Gower, *Leaders of the Crowd*, https://doi.org/10.1007/978-3-030-00383-8_4

With that appreciation in mind, he went to work for a Silicon Valley startup called PeopleSoft, and they flew him around the world to meet with Fortune 500 CFOs to learn best practices in terms of running financials as well as finance and treasury departments. He brought those practices back to PeopleSoft and they were coded into their Enterprise Resource Planning (ERP) program. This is how he learned so much about public companies and raising money on public markets.

After learning how many Fortune 500 companies structure their finance departments and raise capital, he and his brother-in-law started a company called FLAVORx. They flavored medicines so children would be more compliant in taking them. The company is still around. If you go into a pharmacy it's like going to an ice cream store; the kids get to choose whatever flavor they want their medicine to be. In places like CVS or Walgreens or RiteAid you'll see a menu on the wall, Apple to Watermelon. Parents go in there with their sick child and, instead of struggling with them to get them to take medicine they don't like, they ask them what flavor they want their medicine to be. Getting a buy-in from the child as far as taste makes it much more palatable to them, even though it is most definitely not candy. Compliance rates skyrocketed to over 90 percent. This works for the parents because the struggling stops, it works for the kids because they are taking all the medicine and getting better, and it works for the doctors because they don't have parents coming back for secondary medication prescriptions they don't want to write anyway. That company, and funding that company, was the genesis for everything that came after it, and here's why.

They had a product they sold to pharmacies. Their end consumers were parents and children and they needed to raise capital to scale the company. When Woodie originally wanted to raise the first million for the company he went to lawyers and said he wanted to raise money from parents because any time a parent gets their kid to take medicine, the next phone call they make would be to Woodie asking how they can become investors.

He had a list of about 200 people who had asked to become investors in the company and Woodie thought about it this way: if they became investors they would have a vested interest in the outcome of the company. They would be marketing the company through word of mouth and referrals so he wouldn't have to spend a lot of money on doing so himself because this army of vested customers would be doing it for him. Instead, he thought, he could use what he would have spent on marketing to grow the company by putting it into technology or hiring other people for the business.

Of course, his lawyers told him that he clearly knew nothing about the securities laws written in 1933 because: (a) you cannot raise money from people that are non-accredited, and (b) you can't go out there and solicit anyone you don't already know. They told him his idea was completely illegal. He was stunned that laws written back in 1933 were governing how he could raise money today. And the lawyers said, yes, that's exactly how it is.

Woodie asked what his choices were. His advisors told him that he could go to a bank and apply for a loan there, that he could try and raise money from friends and family—which he'd already done a round of—or that he could go to angel investors or VCs. Together with his partners, Woodie decided to explore the VC route. Unlike many other companies that find it hard to get capital, FLAVORx was cash-flow positive, so it was actually very easy for them to find investors.

But Woodie didn't want those investors. He wanted the crowd because he wanted the marketing power that could bring, and he knew he would not get that from the VCs. Nonetheless, he ended up getting three deals, one from Kane Anderson, one from Summit Capital, and one from Concert Capital out of San Francisco, and he had them bid against each other for the best deal. But in the back of his mind, Woodie kept thinking that getting parents as investors was a terrible missed opportunity.

As the company grew, they got more and more calls from parents asking how to become an investor in the company and Woodie had to tell them that he was sorry, but they could not take on that role. He said they had to wait until the company went public through an IPO because he didn't know what else to tell them. In 2007 he sold the company and went on to take a year off to go backpacking around the world. When he returned, he decided he wanted to get into renewable energy.

While getting involved in renewable energy, he was also competing in startup pitch events on the weekends for an app he had created on phones to do instant polling. Developing this app was the result of something that happened when he was raising capital for FLAVORx. They had reported that 90 percent of parents had a problem getting their children to take medicine, and during one of the VC's board meetings, he was asked where that 90 percent number came from. Woodie told the board member it was anecdotal, that they knew it from parents coming into the pharmacy. The executive told him that anecdotal didn't fly because they needed actual market data.

Woodie was dumbfounded. He was being told to hire a market research firm and take time and money they could put into more important things to verify something they already knew was true. So, being of the philosophy that one doesn't argue with the money, and that VCs are smart, he just did as he was told. They hired a market research firm, paid them $50,000, and waited for them to come up with a report.

Three months later they got a beautiful report that confirmed 90 percent of parents had problems getting kids to take medicine. Woodie was completely frustrated with the fact that it took three months to get those results and it occurred to him that, like him, everyone had a phone attached to them, all the time. What happens, he wondered, if people were incentivized to fill out demographic information about themselves if a vendor wants to find out something, like, in their case, when kids have problems taking medicine. He thought that for polling for demographics from parents with kids, they could offer them $50 to complete a survey to get the same results that the market research had conducted. He thought of an app where users would get a text message saying if they completed a survey in the next 30 seconds, they would get $50. All that would be needed then would be quantifying the numbers by determining how many respondents would be needed to have the desired degree of accuracy. In less than five minutes, and having spent significantly less than $50,000, a user could get answers that could be immediately utilized. He built the app and went on to win a weekend startup pitch competition.

And again, he wanted to go out and raise money from not only the people in the room who all wanted to become an investor in this but also friends and family who said they wanted to invest and, importantly, the general public.

He wondered if the laws had changed since he asked about raising money this way for FLAVORx, so he went to talk to lawyers who told him, predictably, that he still could not do it. He thought this was crazy. Kiva was taking off and he could see how they were using this technology to fund entrepreneurs worldwide and, at the time, Kickstarter and Indiegogo were just building their brand, so they were scaling. Woodie could see all the money people were giving to entrepreneurs online and realized that they were not getting any return; they were strictly donation or pre-purchase platforms.

Woodie wondered what would happen if he tweaked the model a little and allowed these same people to become investors in these ideas rather than being donors or pre-purchasing a product. Together with two of his friends from grad school he started ruminating about how crazy these laws were and how antiquated they were, and he just felt that the private capital markets were broken. This was in 2010 at the height of the Great Recession. Woodie decided to take the bull by the horns and do something about it.

Having raised millions of dollars at this point he was familiar with the securities laws. He started learning about them by pulling up the 1933 Securities Act on a computer and going through it backward and forward. He'd also done multiple private offerings.

Together with his friends, he started picking apart the Act and came up with a one-page framework to modify it. Eight things needed to be addressed that would allow them to update the security laws.

This was not deregulation; it was re-regulation.

There were already exemptions out there, with Regulation D in particular. They thought to use the structure of that exemption and to add some other components to allow for online trading of securities. Unbeknownst to Woodie and his team, there were other folk like Jenny Kassan out there on parallel tracks writing letters along the same lines. All he knew was that he was pissed off. He figured that as he lived in DC, he could just walk down to the SEC and do what he needed to do because, well, he was there and if there's one thing he had learned from being an entrepreneur, it's that to get something done, you don't pick up the phone and call or send an e-mail because that goes nowhere, you walk in and you talk to someone face to face.

They wrote this framework and started going around to the people who he knew in DC. Because he lived there, many of his friends worked on the Hill and so he started figuring out who he needed to talk to and how to socialize his agenda. He was introduced to Karen Kerrigan, who ran the Small Business and Entrepreneurship Council because he was talking about the issue at an entrepreneurial event at George Washington University and one of the students heard him speak and said he needed to talk to his boss.

Woodie gave Karen the rundown of what they were doing and she said she was going to put him in touch with key people on the Hill. Preceding this, Woodie and his business partners, Jason and Zak, had gone to the SEC and sat down with them to present their framework. The folk at the SEC said it was interesting, and if it worked it would be great, but the SEC was not in the business of changing any laws, and if they were interested in doing that, they would need to go there, and they pointed at a big white building with a dome on top.

It was literally like that, how insanely pedantic they were, and Woodie pushed back because he knew there were exemptions the SEC could use; Section 3b of the Securities Act, which allowed them to make changes for any de minimis offerings. He told them they had the ability to create any exemptions they wanted, and to add a $1 million offering when their usual offerings were multibillion was definitively de minimis. They weren't interested, and so Woodie trundled over to Capitol Hill.

This is the point at which Woodie likes to recount that his lawyers said he "was unencumbered by knowledge." He and Jason and Zak literally started walking the halls of Congress and, not knowing who to talk to, just walked into any open doors they came to and asked to speak to the person who oversaw job creation. What they learned very quickly was that you never speak to a senator or representative; you speak to the staffers who are the ones that actually get things done in Washington. Woodie didn't know any different and he didn't care. They started speaking to the staffers as they wandered around, asking if they were on Facebook, or did they use LinkedIn or Twitter. Everyone said yes, so they asked if they realized that if someone wanted to raise capital for a startup or a small business in their community where a staffer's representative or senator was their representative, they couldn't do so publicly through customers or the general public by using social media. All the staffers were incredulous that such restrictions could really exist.

All these staffers were from Woodie's generation and so he proceeded to educate them about the laws written in 1933, and this began building staffers' awareness. They focused their attention on the Financial Services Committee. They approached both sides of the aisle and went into every single office, getting them all on board with the one-page framework until eventually it was introduced as a proposal in committee. It exited that committee and when it was introduced as a bill, the lead sponsor was Patrick McHenry. One of the things McHenry said to Woodie and his friends about what they were doing was that they were doing it right. They were showing up, which McHenry said no one does. The only people on the Hill were lobbyists.

Indeed, every time Woodie or one of the others walked into an office, they were asked what lobby firm they were with. When they said they were not with a lobby firm, they were just three entrepreneurs who wanted to do something good for their country and their economy, people were dumbfounded. They just couldn't believe that your average Joe American had walked into their office. That's why Patrick McHenry told them to promise that they were going to continue doing the lobbying because, he said, this is how it gets done. Woodie came to like McHenry. He's a Republican and he advised the team to stay right in the middle and not to get on either side. He told them that they had clearly created a very compelling story about how you can do good for the economy while creating jobs, and that's something that both people on both sides of the aisle could agree upon.

It was great to get these words of wisdom. Woodie came to understand that the minute you indicate a side, people are going to either not get behind it or expect things in return. So their best bet was to just completely stay out of the politics.

And that's what they did. The bill passed the House 407 to 17—a 96 percent approval. It was the highest approved piece of legislation to pass the House that session. Then it went over to the Senate and Woodie continued lobbying there. Woodie and his team went over to the Senate Banking Committee and talked to all the people over there and realized that it was getting stuck in a logjam. Two Democrats and one Republican had picked up the bill and the three of them were struggling to have their bill be the one that was headlined. They weren't necessarily communicating very well with each other and things had slowed down.

So, together with Jason, Woodie decided to write a commonsense compromise which stated everything they were looking for with the House version, merge it all together, and declare that, presto, here it is! And that is exactly what they did. They literally took all four bills, at that point three from the Senate and one that had passed the House, and merged them together, labeling it the "Crowdfunding Commonsense Compromise Bill." Then they walked around to everyone in the Senate and presented it as a compromise and, before they knew it, everyone was saying, "Oh so this is the compromise," to which Woodie would reply, "Yes, this is the compromise."

Everyone literally got behind it and just assumed that something had happened that allowed this compromise to take place because they saw things in it that they were talking about had been incorporated. When it made its way up to the Senate Banking Committee lawyers Woodie sat down with them and went over the entire framework, and something funny occurred.

When they wrote this one-page commonsense document, they drafted it based on what they'd read. Woodie, Jason, and Zak are not lawyers; they are entrepreneurs. Woodie studied political science in school, but that was 20 years earlier. In short, he couldn't remember anything much about how a Bill becomes a Law. So when the Senate Banking Committee was sitting to pass part of the JOBS Act that had been authored based on Woodie, Jason, and Zak's Commonsense Compromise document, the Banking Committee lawyer asked Woodie which law firm had reviewed it. Woodie looked at Jason and the two of them looked at the banking committee lawyers and said, "Law firm? There needs to be a law firm involved?" And the banking committee attorney said again, "Yes, what law firm reviewed this?" When Woodie told him they didn't have a law firm, the poor fellow was stunned. "You're telling me there's a piece of legislation that's going to be voted on in the senate right now that has not been reviewed by a lawyer?!" Woodie told him that it had not. "Is … is that something that's supposed to happen?" he asked.

The lawyer couldn't believe this was happening, so Woodie tried to reassure him that since they had just come over from the House and someone over there had their people looking at it, the bill was probably going to be OK.

It was crazy, Woodie recalls, and it just shows how clearly grassroots the whole effort was.

Woodie met plenty of lobbyists along the way. Woodie, Jason, and Zak spoke to them every day, becoming friends with them, because they asked them questions about what they were doing and how they were doing it. The lobbyists wanted Woodie to hire them, explaining that it would likely take five to ten years and about $5–20 million to conclude the process of passing a bill. Woodie, of course, had no interest in spending five to ten years getting this done, nor could he imagine from where these lobbyists figured they were going to get $5–20 million. They didn't have it. So Woodie just asked the lobbyists for free advice, and if it wasn't forthcoming, he was quite happy not talking to them.

But everyone was surprised that just Woodie and his friends were there and no one else. They didn't come across anyone else who was really working on this until the very end, when it all passed and people were being invited to the White House. The White House told them they needed a statement of support from the industry and they all looked at Woodie to get everyone from the industry together, but neither he nor Jason or Zak knew what other people had been involved.

However, the White House had followed Woodie's progress and helped guide them while they were working on the bill and had talked to the other people working on it as well. Doug Rand at the White House, in particular, had been very valuable throughout the whole process. Woodie says none of it would have happened if it weren't for Doug, who offered Woodie a lot of advice along the way. Woodie felt if the process of getting a bill passed was a chessboard, he was one of the pieces, and that he was being moved and guided by others. He was totally fine with that because he didn't know Washington and Doug did.

Through Doug, Woodie was introduced to all the other people involved and got all of them to sign a letter in support of the Act. But when they were walking the halls they neither came across, nor were introduced to anyone else working on it. Of course, there were many people working on it, or else it wouldn't have happened, but Woodie and Jason and Zak were the ones that showed up constantly. They were the ones talking to people.

In total, Woodie and Jason testified five times in front of House and Senate committees. Those were the only times they realized other constituents were pushing other bills. He only heard about it when they were reading their testimony in those hearings, and that's when he heard about something else people were interested in called the IPO on-ramp that would make it possible for accredited investors to invest in companies online. It made sense that accredited investors should be able to invest online. It all made sense. But Woodie didn't pay attention to any of that, to none of it, because he was only interested in the crowdfunding bill.

In the end, the whole thing passed. The first thing to go into effect was that platforms were able to solicit accredited investors online, but when it came to writing opinion letters to the SEC for this part of the Act, Woodie was quiet because he hadn't worked on that. The White House reached out to him and told him that he needed to be reading everything that was in the JOBS Act and responding to whatever inquiries the SEC had because it was all going to affect Regulation CF. That was the first time Woodie sat down to read all the different parts of the JOBS Act in detail and send his own opinion letters, together with Jason and Zak, as to what they thought about it and how it might impact Regulation CF.

Once the president signed the Act, the SEC picked it up and started the laborious work of promulgating the rules, moving the process from lawmaking to rulemaking. Woodie and his friends went to the White House for the bill signing ceremony in the Rose Garden. That was epic, because how often is anyone able to go to the White House and sit in the Rose Garden, especially if you are there for a bill the president is signing based on an idea you came up with. They were like three schoolboys at this point and then Doug Rand, their friend in the White House, called them and their bubble was burst.

Doug told him at the bill signing ceremony that now was the time the real work began. Woodie didn't understand. The president had just signed the Act into law, but Doug explained that, while this was true, the next phase was the rulemaking phase and that was going to take a while. Woodie needed to be on it with the SEC, so that's when they started meeting with them. This was why he had been advised to pay attention to the rulemaking process, so he could send his thoughts on it.

At that point Woodie had to get the industry coalesced, so, with others, they formed two crowdfunding bodies. Jason and he were not happy that they had to lead it because they wanted to step back from doing any more. They were finished, and didn't want to fly to DC anymore, as they'd spent a lot of their own money just getting the Act passed and weren't getting paid by anyone to continue. They'd just had enough.

But they understood the need to have one voice in the industry and that the voice had to be a lot bigger than just them because they couldn't speak for the industry as a whole. There were a bunch of different platforms coming in. People who wanted to build platforms needed to have their own voice. There were many constituents, and Woodie helped get the Crowdfunding Professional Association formed. The other organization was the Crowdfunding Intermediary Regulatory Advocates that the platforms could use to speak with one voice at the SEC.

It was tough work at the SEC. Woodie sat in on 14 or so meetings to share his thoughts on why there were delays and what could be done to move things along. He was constantly pushing and advocating for them to get it done.

There was resistance from the SEC. As far as Woodie understood, the SEC had never before sent a letter to Congress advising it not to do something, but Mary Jo White penned a letter that said "do not pass Regulation Crowdfunding." She just did not want to see it happening, so when it was signed into law, she was clearly not going to do anything on it while she was still the chair. It is unclear why she was so against it, but she clearly was, and perhaps it's because she didn't understand it. She didn't understand how technology works, she didn't understand how the digital footprint could enable more transparency, how it would be beneficial to the regulators, how it would shed light on what is a very opaque market. Perhaps she was against the regulation because the private capital markets are very opaque and she wanted it kept that way.

She was not alone in her opposition. The state regulators were against it too. Woodie didn't know they were against it, but one time he and Jason and Zak met a woman named Marney who worked for Senator Scott Brown. When they went in to see her, she complained she had such a headache from the last people she'd seen because they had been Woodie's "opponents." Woodie didn't know he had opponents.

Marney told them that, yes, everybody loved them, but that they really did actually have opponents who were vociferously against the JOBS Act and Regulation CF. Seeing Woodie's incredulity, Marney was amused by their naiveté and told them they had stumbled into a world driven by nothing but power and money. She said what they were doing was stripping power away from the state regulators who oversee the private capital markets in their state. These regulators make filing fees on all of this and Woodie was cutting away their power to actually regulate these offerings within their states, and he was taking away the filing fees they make on the offerings.

To underscore the severity of the challenge, Marney asked Woodie if he had ever tried to take a little bit of power away from someone that owns all the power. She told him people don't like losing their power and that was what he and Jason and Zak were doing. Woodie might think in his own mind that what he was doing was just a tiny drop in the ocean of what is for the good of all, but what he did not realize is that someone else owned all the cards and he was asking them to hand over one of those cards, to just to hand it over, and they were saying no. It was their domain and they owned and controlled it, and didn't want anyone else crowding in.

When Woodie originally pushed this through the idea was to have funding portals, because they didn't want to go through state regulation or through broker dealers who were fully licensed under FINRA. Using a funding portal worked because these portals wouldn't have to handle the cash—they could use escrows, which would mitigate the need to be so heavily regulated. It's why FINRA and broker dealers have so much regulation because they're handling funds. The way Regulation CF works is that when the money transferred in a campaign is fully funded, it can go directly from an investor's escrow account to the company without a portal handling the money, so you don't have to worry about a portal going bankrupt and the money disappearing.

The idea was that broker dealers should not be required or mandated because this just raised the cost of capital for these offerings. Woodie thought the way to solve this problem was to use funding portals. They were thinking how to get a Kickstarter type of company, which is not a broker dealer, to allow companies to get on the platform and offer securities as opposed to just selling and taking donations.

In the process of figuring all this out and moving it through Congress and on to the SEC, Woodie came up with the great idea of building his own portal. He and Jason and Zak figured they could become one of the first platforms in the space. They started building it up, calling it the Startup Funding Network. They wanted to be the first to build a platform to support the new law. But as they went into a few offices in Congress, one of the questions they got regularly was whether they were doing this for self-serving reasons, meaning the only reason they were doing this was to directly benefit from the legislation. Woodie and Jason were puzzled. They felt pretty sure that was how Washington literally worked. People do things in their own best interests. No?

And that's how they learned that they were not allowed to build their own platform. They were told that even if it is true that Washington works that way, if they built a platform themselves, they would no longer get help, and legislators would not put their names behind it.

So, they threw out the idea of creating a platform and tried to figure out what to do once the whole thing was done. And that is how they turned into investors. Together with Jason and Zak, Woodie invested in 14 different platforms, including pretty much all the major ones. They have equity in a lot of them, so they are in it for the long haul and are confident that they'll benefit by one or more of these platforms having a big exit at some point.

Woodie and his partners also started Crowdfund Capital Advisors (CCA). The newly formed portals were coming to him and, understanding he was not building a portal and recognizing that he had a name and a face in the industry, were asking him to be on their advisory boards. CCA started working with platforms in the space. Woodie and his team built an education awareness program for entrepreneurs to learn about the opportunity and built a database called CCLEAR—standing for Collect, Clean, Aggregate, and Report—that collects over 150 data points on every single offering taking place online.

Woodie's team see what's happening daily with every single offering, how much money is being committed, and then all that rolls up into what's happening in different industries, what's happening in different regions of the country, what average valuations are, and so on. With that database and the information it yields, governments and the World Bank have hired CCA to help them understand the phenomenon of crowdfunding and to come up with pathways for them to do similar things. They have created roadmaps for Mexico, for Chile, and for the Kingdom of Saudi Arabia. In fact, they do a lot of policy work with governments and regulators globally, totaling some 43 countries so far. Woodie has also gone on to work on expanding the database to deal with the secondary trading of securities. The biggest challenge companies face once they have their securities issued is how to provide liquidity for investors. The only way it can be done currently is to register in all 50 states for an exemption from the state securities laws.

Woodie built a team of lawyers and broker dealers to work with and expanded his database for Regulation CF to capture most of the fields that states want disclosure on in order to qualify for an exemption from state filing so that shares can be sold to individuals in that state for secondary trading. The idea is to allow companies to file only once and yet be compliant with regulations in all 50 states. Woodie's goal is for this to be applicable for any kind of private offering. Any company that wants to provide liquidity for their investors on a secondary market will be able to complete mandatory filings in all 50 states if they want to sell or want their securities to trade all in one place, at one time.

Woodie's team is the first to be doing this because the bureaucracy to get through the hurdle in all 50 states is pretty huge, but he is confident he can pull it off. Considering he was one of the driving forces behind getting a bipartisan bill passed that fundamentally changed the way capital formation works in America, one can only feel optimistic about anything he might turn his attention to.

5

Senate Lead Staffer: Dina Ellis Rochkind

Dina Ellis Rochkind has always had a passion for politics. Both of her parents were those swing voters in Pennsylvania—you know the ones. Her mother was a Republican and her father a Democrat who was a bank examiner for 36 years in the state. "Our dinners," she says, "were heated both literally and figuratively." They talked about politics a lot and, in pursuit of the passion she acquired at home, she went to school to become a lawyer. She decided that she was going to work on Capitol Hill.

After spending 15 years on the Hill, where she got her start on bankruptcy reform working for Congressman George Gekas (R-Pennsylvania), Dina became known as an expert in financial services. She was hired by Congressman Phil Gramm (R-Texas) to work on retail and consumer issues and, at a time of pre-crisis, when banking issues were considered pretty dry and retail finance was considered somewhat controversial, went from Gramm to work for the Bush-Cheney transition team. From there she became Deputy Assistant Secretary of Consumer Affairs and Community Policy with the US Treasury Department. Following that, she went back to the Hill and worked for the House Financial Services Committee as designee for subcommittee for financial institutions and consumer credit, chaired by Senator Spencer Bachus (R-Alabama), who Dina worked for. There she covered consumer issues, as well as banking law. After working with Bachus, Dina went on to Chrysler and was one of the lead lobbyists who worked on rescuing the company.

After Chrysler went into bankruptcy and spun off Chrysler Financial, Dina wanted to get back into financial services. She heard of a position with Senator Pat Toomey (R-Pennsylvania), who had just been elected. Dina was a good fit because she had experience on the Hill and had grown up in Pennsylvania. Sitting in the waiting room waiting to be called in for her interview, Toomey came in, stopped, and asked who she was.

She told him and, although he had already been prepped on her work background, he hadn't known that she was from Pennsylvania. Dina told him that she had grown up in Pennsylvania and had gone to college there. He liked what he heard—"very Pennsylvania"—and began the interview with a series of very hard financial services questions. Dina had spent most of her career in retail and consumer finance, where she hadn't worked so much on some of issues that the banking committees have jurisdiction over—banking insurance, securities, and housing. She had never really worked on the institutional side, although she acquired a sense of what it was when she worked for Chrysler at the time it spun off its finance company.

Dina answered all Toomey's questions successfully and was offered a staff position. She was excited by the opportunity but wanted to check with her husband first—while the position was challenging, so was the salary on offer. Her husband was very supportive, encouraging her to take the position because he thought that Senator Toomey was going to be a player on financial services issues. He had good reason to think so: Toomey's background was as a former derivatives trader who had started up community banks in Pennsylvania, from which he had subsequently separated.

Taking the job with the senator, Dina spent most of her time on institutional issues because, when it comes to securities laws, those issues tend to be more bipartisan and Senator Toomey wanted to get things done.

Senator Toomey had a rough election, unseating 30-year veteran Arlen Specter, and had won with a reputation as a Tea Party outsider. Around a year before the JOBS Act passed, in early 2011, Dina found that most of the financial services staffers in other offices were working to undo parts of Dodd Frank. Each time she began a project she was told that it was already being handled.

Dina was struggling to find a place or project to call her own when opportunity came knocking. The first was when Toomey brought her an article that had appeared in *The Wall Street Journal*. The article outlined how small companies were restricted to having a maximum of 500 shareholders. Once they reached this threshold, they were compelled to take their companies public. Dina had always worked on banking issues. She had no idea that if one tipped over this shareholder limit, one had to become a publicly reporting company—with all the cost, resource, reporting, and time-consuming implications attached. Toomey made it clear that this was a topic to pursue.

Not having much background at the time in securities law, the article might as well have been written in Mandarin Chinese for all it meant to Dina. In an effort to gain a better understanding, her initial thought was to call the American Bankers Association (ABA). It was the first place to start based on her background in banking. The ABA told her that there was a bill, sponsored by former Senator Kay Bailey Hutchison (R-Texas), which was to take care of the shareholder limit for the banks and that they had wanted to see it in Dodd Frank.

This was less controversial because it raised the limit not for all companies, just for banks. Having come from a banking background, Toomey was very familiar with the shareholder limit issue. Initially, his reluctance to support the Kay Bailey Hutchison bill was due to the fact that he wanted to raise the shareholder limit for all companies and not just banks. However, seeing it as a pathway to something bigger, Toomey eventually decided to support the bill—banks first and all businesses later, he thought. Senator Hutchison's bill had almost been included in Dodd Frank, but one of Dodd's staffers who had been concerned about investor protection was successful in keeping it out of the legislation.

While these discussions were continuing, an outside lobbyist representing the biotech industry began visiting Dina: talking about doing something on

Regulation A—which eventually became known as Regulation A+. Being an ally of Toomey's, Congressman David Schweikert's office (R-Arizona) also started calling Dina about making changes to Regulation A. Building further momentum to the idea of reducing regulatory burdens on growth companies, representatives of the New York Stock Exchange joined the discussions on Regulation A+. Their initial interest was in emerging growth companies with what had come to be known as the "on-ramp" provisions that provided for easier IPOs. The on-ramp would ultimately become Title I of the JOBS Act.

Adding impetus behind efforts to ease financial regulations was the biotech industry, which also expressed interest in Regulation A+ and was coordinating with the National Venture Capital Association to the same end. It took some time for Dina to be able to make progress on this because she and Toomey were intent on having bipartisan support for every piece of legislation that was introduced.

Enter Jim DeMint (R-South Carolina). DeMint was a senator who was known for helping a number of Tea Party people get elected. However, he was not known for being a legislator. Dina was working with his office and, at the end of the day, DeMint wound up introducing things that went further—and without Democrats, which helped Toomey appear to be more reasonable. Toomey very much wanted to be constructive and get things done, but Dina was having a hard time with the capital formation bills, trying to get Democrats on board.

Coincidentally, however, Senator Jon Tester (D-Montana) was assigned at the time to the Subcommittee on Economic Policy. Senator Tester's subcommittee was holding a hearing on capital formation and welcomed Senator Toomey to sit in, even though Toomey wasn't a member of that subcommittee. After the hearing, Dina discovered through Tester's staff that Toomey had met with Tester and decided that the easiest starting point for capital formation was going to be Regulation A; it was bipartisan and there had been various rumblings out of the White House indicating support of these same Regulation A changes.

The benefit of improvements to Regulation A for the biotech and venture capital industries, supported as they were by the New York Stock Exchange, was facilitation of the IPO process. This meant more companies could go public. They thought it would be easier for them to raise capital by getting out from under some of the regulatory burden, and by finding more efficient ways of executing exits from investments.

Part of Dina's responsibility was to write the bill that would be voted on in the Senate. As a lot of the negotiation on Regulation A+ had already been done in the House, though she probably wouldn't have written it exactly as it was in its current state, and though a somewhat uncommon process, she found it expedient to take the House bill and to copy it for the Senate.

This also helped in winning SEC acquiescence, with opposition only coming from the fringes and some other more progressive members. The opposition wasn't so impactful, and the bill proceeded. The SEC did not really speak on the Senate side regarding the JOBS Act except to oppose it at the very end. Even then they sent their head of corporate finance up to the Hill, whose most memorable comment was that the Regulation A+ provision "was meaningless but not scary."

The SEC didn't think it would do anything because Regulation A already existed, and the Senate was just broadening it a bit. It was a small bill—it was the easiest to work on—and neither the SEC, or Dina, nor anyone else in the Senate thought it would have much impact other than to see a small uptick in the number of IPOs hitting the market. The SEC ended up sending a letter to the Senate opposing the entire JOBS Act, and the biggest opponent to Regulation A+ was the National Association of Securities Administrators Association (NASAA), who wanted to protect their own independence at the state level.

Far more impactful, everyone thought, was going to be the increasing shareholder limits; the biggest coalition was on the shareholder side. This formed the engine for the entire JOBS Act in the Senate because, without increases in these limits, none of the other capital formation bills would function efficiently.

As stated earlier, Toomey wanted to do this for all businesses, not just for banks, as had originally been contemplated. One day, Dina got a call from the Philadelphia Chamber of Commerce. They called having seen that Senator Toomey had been on the shareholder limit bill: the Kay Bailey Hutchison bill. The Chamber told Dina that they had a member who was very interested in seeing shareholder limits increased. It was a nonbank business and therefore unlikely to benefit, she told the caller. However, because Toomey was interested in raising the limits for everyone, Dina was curious to know who the client was, and it turned out to be Wawa, an iconic East Coast chain of convenience stores. Wawa is well known for being an oasis for folk going to the Jersey shore. This love of brand is almost cult-like. Wawa is very popular, so when Dina heard it was them, she realized there may be a hook upon which to hang the bill. More on this later.

That said, the first people to come into Dina's offices were representatives from two private trading share platforms—SecondMarket headed up by Barry Silbert and Gate Global Impact headed up by Vincent Molinari.

Both were lobbying on behalf of shareholder limits. They had a lot of letters from startups who were also supportive: startups like Gilt Group, for example, among others. Curiously for Dina, she was not lobbied by Facebook and was in shock when the JOBS Act was briefly called "The Facebook Bill." Incidentally, Twitter reached out to her, but only far down in the process.

At SecondMarket Barry Silbert together with Mark Murphy were handling public relations (PR) for their platform, and Vincent Molinari at Gate Global Impact did some lobbying together with outside agencies. They were effective and well informed, though they had not previously thought about the older companies that wanted to grow. They had only thought of startups and trading platforms, but had never thought that these older, established players would be interested.

So that's how it got built. It was Wawa and other private companies on Main Street like Wegmans and WL Gore that were the catalyst for the whole thing. Now Dina needed a Democrat to sign on for Toomey to introduce the bill.

Pennsylvania had a lot of old companies in it that were running up against the limit. Dina wound up going to Tom Carper (D-Delaware). He was a good option because WL Gore, the maker of Goretex, was headquartered in Delaware and had a plant in Pennsylvania. Though Carper was no longer on the Banking Committee, he had always been an active player on financial services issues. Toomey and Carper shared the same media market that they could leverage for mutual benefit by cooperating on a bipartisan bill, and with Delaware-based Wawa stores also in the mix, it made sense to try to get Carper on the shareholder legislation. Carper was known for working across the aisle and, combined with his prior banking experience, it was assumed that he would be sympathetic.

He agreed, and the bill was renamed Toomey-Carper, while Regulation A+ was called Tester-Toomey. Toomey agreed to a second billing on the latter: the Democrats were in power at the time. But because the shareholder limit issue was deeply connected to the state of Pennsylvania, Dina felt it was important Toomey's name be first. There was also some concern about him getting beat up back home and this would help mitigate that risk.

The process of finalizing the new limit began. The Senate was more aggressive than the House, where they were down to 1000 shareholders. Dina took it to 2000, excluding employees, and then the House took it back down to 1000. Interestingly, a progressive Democrat, George Miller (D-California), offered an amendment to the bill on the floor when the JOBS Act was being considered in the House, and their version was 2000, but with only 500 who could be non-accredited. At that time, Dina didn't think the non-accredited limitation was a big deal because she never contemplated that the bills would be for retail investors. No-one was thinking about crowdfunding in the stricter non-accredited sense, and with Toomey's banking experience, the focus had always been on accredited investors. The decision was that it was more important going up high on the number rather than shoot for more non-accredited.

The limit wound up at 2000 from an original cap of 500, with only 500 non-accredited, excluding employees, and as it was bipartisan and because WL Gore, among others, were in his home state, Carper came on board. This was important because Carper was, by far, the biggest supporter of the JOBS Act on the Democrat side.

With Wawa, Dina had brought Main Street to the table to complement the venture capital and secondary markets lobbyists, and she took the Main Street contingency and grew it; Wawa, WL Gore, Wegmans, and others all came together, bringing lobbyists on board to add further impetus, and the coalition grew.

On-Ramp, 506(c), Regulation Crowdfunding

There was a task force that was informally set out by the Treasury Department called an IPO Task Force headed by Kate Mitchell, chairman of the National Venture Capital Association (NVCA), although it was the NVCA and New York Stock Exchange that were really the faces of it for Dina. After Tester's and Toomey's offices introduced the Regulation A+ bill, which was the first bill in the Senate, the first capital formation bill, the two offices became known as the capital formation offices.

Representatives of the task force came in one day and presented the IPO on-ramp proposal. Almost like a road show. Dina really liked the IPO on-ramp. She felt that they had a chance to get it done without opposition from the accounting firms because they were going after smaller companies in terms of the regulatory relief to help them in going public. But Tester's office called Dina after the meeting to tell her that he was not going to be able to sign on. He was facing a fight for re-election in Montana, which is always a swing state, and the bill looked too much like Wall Street. Again, Dina needed a Democratic co-sponsor.

It turned out that Senator Chuck Schumer (D-New York) wanted to do it with Toomey. Schumer was the lead Democrat in the Senate and, at the time, was the second most powerful Democrat in the Senate as the Whip. It was no secret that he hadn't really wanted Toomey to have the Pennsylvania seat in the first place, so the idea of working with his office was a bit surreal. However, Dina knew that Schumer was a man who got things done, and this was cause for optimism. The only thing that Schumer's staff asked Dina to pull out of the bill was one of the regulatory provisions giving emerging growth companies relief from the conflict mineral requirements of Dodd Frank. The conflict mineral requirements were the last item in Dodd Frank and were designed to ensure supply chains had ethical sources. Dina was open to this request because conflict minerals was just a distraction. With that settled, and some tweaking to get the language right, Toomey did a press conference with Senator Schumer.

The IPO on-ramp comprised the bulk of the pages of the JOBS Act and, yet, the other parts are an interesting story too. There was a guy who worked on the House Financial Services Committee called Walton Liles and Dina got to know him because he had, coincidentally, worked at Goodwin Procter law firm, where Dina's brother-in-law is a partner. Liles had worked there as an associate, was from Alabama, and came to the Hill, where he worked for Congressman Spencer Bachus (R-Alabama). Bachus was the chairman of the committee where Dina had previously also worked.

Liles was the guy who was working on a lot of the Act's provisions and Dina got together with him because she wanted to know who the constituencies were on the other bills. They met up and Liles told her that to write Regulation D, 506(c), he had gone through the transcripts and the minutes from the Small Business Advisory Committee at the SEC and that the recommendations he was writing into the bill came up over and over again. In other words, Liles had not been lobbied on it. Contrary to her expectations, the hedge fund industry was not lobbying at all and it left Dina wondering who wanted it.

Now, the House typically moves before the Senate, so it was like this: the House had a Regulation A bill and the Senate had a Regulation A bill. The House had a shareholder limit bill and Dina's office was interested in shareholder limits, but wanted a somewhat different version. When they were talking about emerging growth companies, the focus was on relief from Sarbanes-Oxley 404 B. The House was trying to increase the limit on who had to comply with 404 B and was running against opposition from the accounting firms.

Dina didn't want to go that route. Instead she and her people introduced the IPO on-ramp bill and the House copied that. The House also had a Regulation D bill and a crowdfunding bill and was attempting to pass each of the bills separately—other than the IPO on-ramp because that was the Senate's first. But there were some conflicts on the shareholder limit bill which caused it to stop moving for a while. Then the House started to pass bills individually and overwhelmingly, and so there was pressure for them to pass it in the Senate. Adding to this momentum—the White House was weighing in on a couple of things.

The White House was supportive of the Regulation A bill, and was also supportive of, though never enthusiastic about the exact language, the notion of crowdfunding. The crowdfunding piece has its own complicated story. On the House side Patrick McHenry (R-North Carolina) had the crowdfunding bill. He was known as an active player on capital formation and fintech issues, and had a constituent reason because Pabst Blue Ribbon wanted it and was headquartered in his home state. The crowdfunding bill in the Senate was having a tug of war between interested parties over the matter of consumer protection. Everyone was debating the extent of investor protection needed in the crowdfunding provisions.

Dina felt that anything that tied all the capital formation bills together—the IPO on-ramp, shareholder limits, and Regulations A, D, and CF—would be helpful as she tried to build bipartisan support. She didn't know if it was going to get passed in the current Congress or in the next Congress; she was just trying to build the best product she could and get as much support as she could.

She had no idea that things were going to move as fast as they eventually did.

There were all these disparate bills floating in the capital formation ecosystem on Capitol Hill and, at some point, they were all brought together by Eric Cantor (R-Virginia), House Majority Leader. Cantor was the guy who was thought of as the "guy tied to Wall Street" and he prided himself as being involved in financial services issues. He packaged all the bills, and he and his staffer Mike Ference named it the Jumpstart Our Business Startups Act, aka the JOBS Act. "Brilliant," recalls Dina. An acronym no one could resist.

The hard part for Dina was to get the Senate to pass the same exact bill as the House, thus avoiding a call to conference. Dina was concerned that if it had gone to conference, the result would have been meaningless. To mitigate this risk, Dina tried to replicate what had come out of the House as closely as possible. In the meantime, the SEC sent a letter up opposing every piece of the bill. Toomey was scheduled to appear on national television the next day. Dina worked through the night, addressing all the SEC objections to the provisions of the Act. The SEC's concerns were ignored and the Act passed.

Most Impactful Component

Dina thought that raising the shareholder limit was going to have the biggest impact because it was so hard for a private company to go public. At the time, if a company was cash-flow positive, it was not worth the trouble to go public. Dina felt it would be impossible to change a lot of the things in the public markets because of all the politics involved. But, she thought, if the shareholder limits could be raised, this would facilitate companies' capital raising while avoiding the quagmire of entering public markets by helping them to stay private.

Additionally, pre-JOBS Act, there was a ban on all general solicitation. Investors had to know someone, be tied into wealthy people or tied into groups. They would have to "know people" to be solicited for any kind of anything and sponsors couldn't just go out on Facebook or advertise at all. In short, there was a complete ban on general solicitation that was lifted globally across all the bills that went in to form the JOBS Act.

But no one was lobbying specifically for lifting the prohibition on general solicitation. No one was coming to the Hill and talking about what the impact would be. No one contemplated the impact. In short, the lifting of the prohibition on general solicitation, while being possibly the most impactful of all components of the JOBS Act, was among the least contemplated and the least understood.

And of course, it's the single biggest thing for the real estate industry. Allowing general solicitation is what changed everything, and everything else is mere detail. The single biggest impact of the JOBS Act on real estate is that sponsors could now advertise. The regulations—Regulations A, D, and CF—are all dependent on individual circumstances; the transformational change on real estate was general solicitation.

And no one was lobbying for it, so no one was focused on it.

One thing that tipped Dina off about it happened at the end of the process. The Investment Company Institute (ICI) that represents the mutual fund industry opposed the provision. One cannot do general solicitation for mutual funds, but the JOBS Act helped hedge funds to compete with mutual funds. When the ICI came out in opposition, it was late in the process. Too late, but it was the only thing that gave Dina a hint that this helped hedge funds. And the hedge fund industry had stayed quiet because they knew that anything they supported—anything seen to be representing Wall Street—would likely be opposed. It was a really big win for the hedge fund industry because before investors had to know someone and be invited to a deal. Typically, these were small groups in wealthier cities. By permitting advertising, the entire country was opened, thereby democratizing the ability to raise capital. The benefit to hedge funds was tremendous: the investor pool expanded nationwide.

The Lobbyists

Being focused largely on accredited investors, with her coalition of interested parties weighing in on Regulations A and D, shareholder limits, and on-ramp provisions, Dina wasn't particularly focused on Regulation CF. There was no sophisticated lobbying effort for it. But there was one particularly credible guy for Dina. Woodie Neiss showed up, and he made sense. He owned a company called FLAVORx and his story was particularly compelling. Understanding that things don't usually move in a void in the financial services space, Dina asked Woodie who other than him wanted Regulation CF. It would be easier, she thought, for her to make progress if she had somebody who wanted it in Congress. Dina was also concerned about keeping Toomey safe from getting attacked by groups back in Pennsylvania.

The best way to do this, she figured, was to stay away from retail investors. Neither she nor Tester's people were thinking Regulation A+ was going to affect retail investors. Of course, it would eventually have a huge impact on them. Another thing that was certainly never intended was that while making it easier to solicit investors by getting rid of the ban on general solicitation, the SEC chose to create a higher hurdle in determining accreditation.

Many of the lead players on the JOBS Act on the Hill were very frustrated by the fact that the SEC was apparently trying to undermine the Act's intent. There were repeated letters from Toomey, Thune, McHenry, and others who were involved in the JOBS Act, pushing back against the SEC's resistance. By making it harder to evidence accredited status, the SEC threw a light on the standard itself. The rules relating to what defines an accredited investor were promulgated in 1982. In those days interest rates on bank deposits were 12 percent and a mortgage was 20 percent plus. The Dow broke through the stratospheric 1000 level. It was a different era. And the standard has not, for the most part, changed since that time. Whether you earned $200,000 in 1982 or in 2018, you are classified as being accredited. The underlying principle for the standard is that wealth or income can serve as a proxy for intelligence or education.

For Dina, there is no standard other than an age hurdle for people that gamble, and gambling certainly can be much more damaging. So why is there such a stringent hurdle for investing? Particularly, she thought, if you're going through a professional, especially at a time when more companies are staying private because of the way the JOBS Act is designed, should regulations prevent people from having a more diverse set of investments? It's so hard to go public now that investors are not as diverse as they might otherwise be. This is not supportive of stability in the broader economy. Since the standard started to get attention, the SEC has begun looking at whether they should change it; some suggest total elimination.

From Dina's perspective there have been a couple of unexpected results to come out of the JOBS Act. The first is that Regulation A+ was applied to retail investors and has been significantly more impactful than people imagined it was going to be. Even though Regulation A+ was described as "not scary but meaningless," the industries that have grown up around it have done so with a level of excitement far beyond expectations.

As someone who was a novice to securities laws, the JOBS Act process and ensuing impact made Dina realize that the Act had merely scratched the surface; that although the United States has the deepest and most liquid capital markets in the world, we nevertheless have disclosure and investor protection laws that needed modernizing. There needs to a concerted effort to modernize our securities laws, rooted as they are in a Depression-era economy, to better fit with the Information Age.

6

Investor Protections: Andy Green

Andy Green is a securities lawyer by training but was also someone who had a background and an interest in living and working in China. After law school he went to work as a securities lawyer in the Hong Kong offices of a prominent New York law firm involved in corporate securities deals. The work was very interesting and he felt he was on the cutting edge of global finance in the mid-2000s.

But he had other passions, as well, namely politics and public policy. When the global financial crisis hit, Barack Obama was the elected president, record numbers of Democrats resided in both Congress and the Senate, and Andy decided to go to Washington DC to get involved in public policy. Lo and behold, and very fortunately, he was matched up with Jeff Merkley (D-Oregon), a freshman senator who had joined the senate banking committee and was looking for somebody with an understanding and background in financial markets given what had just happened in the housing markets during the financial crisis.

Merkley also wanted somebody who had a bit of an outsider's take and had not already been captured by the DC machinery, so Andy, coming from Hong Kong, fit those two criteria. In addition, being from San Francisco (which is in southern Oregon, as Andy jokingly told Senator Merkley) expanded his outsider appeal even further. Andy joined Merkley's team in early 2009. For the first couple of years he worked extensively on the response to the financial crisis and the country's largest banks and some nonbank lenders brush with failure that nearly led to the meltdown of the economy. The various risks and abuses to consumers and homeowners were all things at the top of his agenda, but one part of that was the access to capital and to credit challenges that small businesses faced.

Small businesses of all types were facing tremendous challenges in terms of obtaining the lending they needed. The banks and lenders that had been financing them were under strain and the value of their collateral was dropping through the floor. Their customers and their cash flow were being squeezed by the recession and the financial crisis in general. It was a really difficult time for small businesses around the country, and because they hadn't caused the financial crisis and instead were victims just like everyone else, most people in DC were looking for something to improve the situation.

Andy started working on these issues as early as 2009, although crowdfunding did not come to the fore until 2011, when it was one of a number of ideas that started to percolate up through the conversation in Washington DC. Andy paid particular attention when he started to hear about it. Some members on the House side were talking about it and had drafted a related bill. During this period it felt like social media was growing rapidly, and the idea that one could begin to use the information obtained via social media to help make better decisions across all aspects of life was an emerging sensibility at that time, if not a prevalent one. Additionally, the Obama administration had a very strong pro-technology, pro-Silicon Valley feel to it. This occurred long before the later scandals of Russian bots and other things that made people develop a little more skepticism toward the wisdom of the crowd.

This was in the ether when everyone on the Hill was looking for new ideas. At that time Andy just happened to stumble across a small rally in a Senate park that staffers walk through being held by Sherwood "Woodie" Neiss and Jason Best and a couple of other advocates who were small business folk. He approached them and struck up a conversation, trying to get more information about what they were pushing and why they were so excited about it. As he learned more he discussed it with Merkley, pointing out the idea was generating a lot of excitement. Andy was intrigued with how to tap the potential of evolving technology and transparency in a way that would better enable small businesses to match up with investors who might be ready or willing to take appropriate levels of risk and therefore get capital to the small businesses that needed it.

Andy was cautious, though. The dialogue at that time tended to be centered in a kind of techno-utopia coming out of Silicon Valley that seemed to be promulgating that technology would solve all problems. Andy was skeptical and had a growing sense that it just wasn't true. Even the best uses of technology have certain downsides and negative impacts or unintended consequences, but the prevailing narrative seemed to gloss over that and portray the sense that technology was a panacea. One of the things very much at the forefront of Andy's mind throughout the process was that using technology best practices opened up opportunities if approached thoughtfully, with the recognition that risks to ordinary people need to be ameliorated to the best of one's ability. He saw this understanding and sentiment echoed in the minds of Senator Merkley and others, and it was certainly also at the forefront of President Obama's mind as well as that of the White House. Possessing this mindset is how Andy ended up working very closely with the White House.

History reminds us that raising money from ordinary investors poses some risks of outright fraud and theft, no matter the dollar amount involved. There is a good amount of risk involved with investing. Even if the issuer is not misleading and does not intentionally try to defraud the investor, there is always an inherent risk that the company they've invested in will not succeed and they will lose their money. Just plain old risk. Andy and his team wanted to bake into whatever they did a reasonable level of investor protections, so the potential for market development was supported by the trust necessary to bring capital to the market.

The principle driving this approach was that investors *are* the capital. Investors must trust the system and have confidence that they'll be able to manage the process and evaluate the risks. They must know that the market is largely free of fraud, so the risk of being misled is minimal. If they aren't sure of these things, they won't show up and put in capital. Sure, there would be risks; people would sometimes make money, and sometimes they'd lose money, but that's OK.

Moving the idea of crowdfunding along in what was ultimately the Regulation CF part of the JOBS Act was this basic bargain the bill's original sponsor, Patrick McHenry, put forward: "Hey, it's a relatively small amount of money, so let's let the market do what it wants and it will sort itself out. People won't lose much." Andy wasn't comfortable with that. He understood the premise, but felt it needed to be tightened. He wanted to put a few more specifics in there, and so rewrote the draft McHenry's team had prepared, retaining some components of the original 1933 and 1934 Acts.

McHenry's team had built some exemptions from the 1933 and 1934 Acts that Andy wanted to see put back in. There were a couple of items in particular. One was that an issuer should include a basic description of the business, and two, that when the issuer signed on the dotted line, they were assuming a basic level of liability that what they said in their disclosures was the truth. These were two very basic 1933 Act requirements that Andy thought imperative to include. (For those who don't know, the 1933 Securities Act set out basic federal anti-fraud protection requirements of corporate disclosure for companies trying to raise money from the public.) The other thing Andy wanted to make sure happened was that the regulations not be overly complicated, so it would be relatively easy for a small business coming to the market to raise capital.

But he felt that the more important touchpoint for investor protection related to the licensed professionals who had traditionally marketed companies to the public, and from an historical perspective, these professionals were the broker dealers regulated by the 1934 Securities Exchange Act. Andy and his colleagues decided that the full 1934 Act regulatory regime pertaining to broker dealers wasn't necessary. They wanted a very light version of this, envisioning the role to be taken instead by dedicated companies on dedicated platforms powered by technology and algorithms, and their ability to do this on a very simple straightforward basis.

To achieve this objective, Andy recognized that someone wanting to trade in crowdfund securities would need to do a few things to protect investors. If they wanted to be broker dealers, that was fine: they could follow all the associated rules. But if they didn't want to be a broker dealer, they didn't have to be; they could be a "funding portal" instead, which was a term Andy came up with.

He said there needed to be some oversight of the funding portals by the SEC that required them to keep basic record books to ensure an issuer was not engaged in money laundering or terrorist financing. The funding portal would have to do a little "kicking of the tires" to make sure there was actually somebody on the issuer side of the transaction who wasn't a complete fraudster.

The portals would not be expected to guarantee the company issuing money on the portal's platform was going to do great, but they would be the first round of fraud protection for the public. If Andy and his team were to draft the legislation properly, the public would have greater trust that the folk on the portal's platform were vetted players whom they could evaluate to determine whether their deals were good or bad without concern about legitimacy.

Those two things, basic disclosure by the companies and a basic kicking of the tires approach with some oversight by the SEC of funding portals, were envisioned as the foundation of this light, but tailored, regime. Andy thought it had some reasonably robust protections, so the market could develop some investor trust because people would be putting money at risk.

Andy also evaluated and worked on all the other capital formation bills contained in the JOBS Act. There were other ideas out there in the mix that ended up not being included in the legislation. Andy was never really happy with the entirety of the JOBS Act, and, indeed, Senator Merkley voted against it. Andy felt there were many portions of the JOBS Act that were problematic for ordinary investors and ordinary folk.

One example was the provision that exploded the number of shareholders a company could have and still be a nonpublic company. This went from 500 to 2000, and even more with certain technicalities. This doesn't sound like a whole lot, but the way shareholders are counted ends up meaning that potentially hundreds of thousands, if not millions, of people could be baked into a company's shareholder base. Andy was concerned that this would seriously undermine IPOs and the idea that there would be more companies going public, which, whether you thought the JOBS Act achieved it or not, was the ostensible purpose of Title I of the JOBS Act. But by increasing the shareholder limit, the Act would actually just be supercharging existing trends in the market where private capital raising was becoming the dominant form of raising capital for companies at every step and at every size of an entity.

There were other parts of the Act that also concerned Andy. Perhaps the most serious problem with the JOBS Act was the deregulation of general solicitation—the ability to advertise an offering. General solicitation is one of the touchstones of what a public offering is and what triggers the full oversight of the securities laws and all the requirements that everything be disclosed, fairly and in one place, and that there's liability for what an issuer says. The JOBS Act dials that back and says, *Hey, if you're just offering to a small set of people who have a lot of money, you can still advertise to the entire world. And you know, if somebody calls up or sends their money and they lose that money, that's their problem.*

Well, the problem with lessons from history is that they don't work out very well for a lot of people, and the risks to the general public really do outweigh the benefits derived by good companies that want to raise money. General solicitation just opens the door to too much risk of fraud, and too much risk of abuse. So that was and continues to be a serious concern with the JOBS Act for Andy.

This leads into concerns he also had with Regulation A+. There is a way of looking at the JOBS Act, which Commissioner Kara Stein (who was Andy's colleague working for Senator Jack Reed (D-Rhode Island) and who Andy later worked for at the SEC) has talked about, which approaches it as a sliding scale, where the degree of regulations imposed on capital formation is related to the amount of capital company being raised—that is, the more money a company needs, the tighter the regulations. This way of thinking about the Act says you try to look at where a company is in its life cycle and in terms of its size as well as how much money was to be raised and from whom it would be raised. Applying differing degrees of regulations depending on the answers to these questions is a sensible approach, but not one Andy thinks was achieved.

The Act moved in the right direction, but Andy thinks there's still more work to do. At the most highly regulated end of the scale is full-on registration of a company for a public offering—an IPO. This happens for usually large companies with a lot of revenues. They're listed on the major exchanges—the New York Stock Exchange, Nasdaq, and so on—have $1 billion or more in revenue, and are raising $200 or $300 million and upward.

That kind of large scale comes with full requirements for reporting every detail of the business because what the securities laws do is stand in the shoes of a sophisticated investor. Let's say you're Warren Buffett. You can go kick the tires on even the largest companies because the big companies will answer your phone call. They want to take your money. But if you are an average investor, the company is not going to answer your phone call. Even if they do take your call, what they tell you may or may not be true. The securities law says, no, we're going to make the issuing company disclose to everyone equally as though they were talking to Warren Buffett and telling him all about the assets they own or their intellectual property (IP), how many workers they have, what their business plan is and what the risks are, and so on.

That's the full offering at the top of the scale, and once a company is public, it's subject to annual reporting under the 1934 Act. It's expensive, but the company gets a lot of money out of it and can raise an unlimited amount from the public.

Then the sliding scale of stock offerings drops down to the point where it comes to the land of public versus private. On the public side there's Regulation A, to which the JOBS Act added Regulation A+ and Regulation CF. Here's the key difference between them. Down in the mini-public offerings of Regulation A used to be a regime meant to raise $5 million or so. An issuer could go to the public and each investor could put in as much as they wanted. Using Regulation A, however, meant the issuer had to get the approval of all the state regulators where they were going to offer, whereas a full-blown IPO is national in scope.

Regulation A+ ended up being a compromise. It said the cap would be raised to $50 million and would pre-empt the state regulators—which was something that the folk at the SEC were very concerned about. In Regulation A+ there would be a smaller prospectus, a smaller disclosure document, and a lighter liability regime. Regulation A+ is somewhere in the middle of crowdfunding, which was designed to be up to $1 million, and a full public offering where the ceiling is unlimited. A $50 million offering probably doesn't get a company listed on the New York Stock Exchange, which has higher thresholds for listing, but even so, $50 million is not a trivial offering.

The crowdfunding bill had an even smaller, lighter set of disclosures. The bill pre-empted state regulators, but Regulation CF offerings create a national market with smaller raises and a smaller set of liabilities.

The other approach to raising money is in the private markets using Regulation D. Here you have to be accredited, meaning an investor who has demonstrated they've got money in the bank or are in a qualified business. In private markets the requirements of public disclosure don't apply because it is presumed that an accredited investor knows what they are doing and can take the risks because either they're in that business or they have enough money that if they lost it, the state would not care from a public policy perspective.

However, the financial crisis of 2008–2009 actually suggests that thesis doesn't really work because there are a lot of folk who were accredited and sophisticated investors who made a lot of bad investments and lost a lot of money which helped fuel the financial crisis. Even so, overwhelming amounts of capital in Silicon Valley is raised today via these private markets of angel and venture capital investors, and even hedge funds and wealthy people put money into a company and can demand whatever disclosures they want.

Today, private markets dwarf public markets: they are the dominant markets for raising money. They don't dwarf public markets in terms of market cap, but in terms of the capital that is raised on a yearly basis. Private markets are extremely important; you have to be a wealthy person to play in that space. Yet they're largely unregulated, and that's what makes Regulation D so important. One of the theories behind crowdfunding was that if public markets can be opened up in a way that uses technology and is safe, this private network world of Regulation D could be democratized a little bit and some of the companies that might otherwise go to angel and VCs for their capital could actually raise money from the public.

There are nuances involved. If you're a company with a really exciting idea or a really exciting IP that you don't want to get stolen, you might choose to go private regardless of whether crowdfunding exists. So there are some business arguments as to why crowdfunding itself is limited in terms of its potential to democratize finance. Within this private market space the JOBS Act did include a small provision that said we're going to have a lighter regulatory oversight on reducing the broker dealer regulation of platforms offering basic crowdfunding offerings, but only to accredited investors. Platforms would be permitted to do a kind of high wealth network approach to crowdfunding, but only in the confines of private groups. Another tweak in the JOBS Act that facilitated this was the large-scale deregulation of general solicitation, which said issuers could advertise at the Super Bowl if they wanted to; as long as they were only taking money from accredited investors, regulators would not care.

This was included as one of the provisions of the JOBS Act; that it's OK for a company to advertise their presence to the world as long as they only acted within private groups and established digital relationships with self-verified, accredited investors rather than meeting them in person.

In the summer of 2014, Andy migrated from Merkley's office to the SEC when an opportunity came to work for Commissioner Kara Stein on her staff. The SEC has five commissioners, and at that time the chair person was Mary Jo White. Traditionally, there is the majority party, the president's party has three, and the other party has two. At that time President Obama had Mary Jo White and two Democratic commissioners. Commissioner Stein was one of those democrats and Andy was advising her on all the rulemaking, all the enforcement cases that come through the SEC and that the commissioner had to vote on. Andy was thrown into the middle of whatever was going on there, including derivatives regulations, working on aspects of asset manager oversight, helping to implement the Dodd Frank Act, and coming out of the financial crisis. He also worked on corporate disclosures and small business capital JOBS Act issues.

It took almost two years for JOBS Act rules to be promulgated. While many people think this was an unusually long time, Andy discovered it was actually a relatively short amount of time, since it's not unusual for things to take two years from when they are passed into law to when the rules are finalized by the SEC.

During the process of writing the various capital formation bills, Andy was aware that real estate was a possible beneficiary of the Act, as it came up in discussions. There were folk who shared ideas for how the Act was going to be used in real estate transactions to rebuild hard-hit communities. But, Andy says, the Act and its component bills were principally designed to work for small companies. The Act was not designed to facilitate real estate, though it certainly wasn't designed to preclude real estate. Andy and his team did exclude certain types of companies saying that the Act was expressly not for hedge funds but that it didn't limit the type of company that could raise money because defining what a small business was and was not gets very complicated.

The sense was that coming right off the financial crisis and the housing boom and bust, real estate was not a sector that needed crowd investments in any way. Certainly not for commercial real estate. If there was a focus on real estate at the time, it was to help people afford to buy a home. The government wanted people to be able to get affordable loans, a good solid 30-year fixed-rate mortgage, the old American Dream loan. Crowdfunding was not meant to raise money for real estate investors nor was it designed for that purpose.

Commissioner Stein had a vision for capital markets that she laid out in a speech in Los Angeles in 2014 and that Andy helped advance. Stein wanted to see fund-raising marketplaces designed to have a scale of different venues for raising money that were aligned with the risks and the opportunities and the needs of companies and investors at different scales and the needs of the capital-raising process. Participants in the capital markets debate were "getting far too wrapped around the axle," says Andy, in trying to figure out a one-size-fits-all solution. The thesis was too binary: you're either in or you're out; you're covered by certain things or you're not covered by certain things. Andy was sympathetic to Commissioner Stein's view that capital formation needed to adapt to the Information Age. With the amount of data driving the marketplace, with the scope and scale and speed that technology offers, a market needed to be crafted that drew upon these circumstances.

Diversity of businesses and people and the services offered in the economy could not all be satisfied by one super-solution; instead, a scaled approach to regulation was needed. For this reason the prospect of introducing crowdfunding was a really exciting development, provided legislators remained mindful of the risks; crowdfunding should be a place where whoever shows up—be they mom and pop or more sophisticated investors—they're going to get a fair shake and be able to understand what they're getting out of this marketplace.

Andy wanted to explore the possibilities of trying different things and making adjustments. Crowdfunding, that part created by Title III of the JOBS Act, was only one part of the scale of opportunities the Act and other parts of the SEC regulations and laws created. Together the various parts of the Act created a set of scaled tailoring, but he didn't think they went far enough; there were things he would have done differently. That said, one of the most exciting things about the JOBS Act is that when people talk about crowdfunding, they don't always zero in on Title III's Regulation CF, where there is a $1 million cap and lower investor limits, and so on. There's potential to call regulation A+ a kind of crowdfunding because it includes general solicitation and allows non-accredited investors to participate. Indeed, there are even crowdfunding-type provisions in Regulation D, in the private market space, most particularly in the general solicitation rule. What distinguished crowdfunding, as Andy helped to write it in its literal form, as defined in Regulation CF, as opposed to other forms of investing, was the idea that there would be a very limited amount of money that would have less regulatory protections because it would match the amount of money that's at play. The vision was to craft something where the regulations or laws would be responsive to market conditions and be nimble, able to make adjustments intrinsically. The process of implementing this vision was to design something, watch how it worked, see how it could be improved, and if problems emerged too quickly, move to shut it down and make other adjustments as needed.

That's one of the lessons Andy and others who made the rules wanted to keep in mind, certainly in the tiny area of Title III, Regulation CF. Andy was not quite as sanguine about the other parts the JOBS Act. There's absolutely no doubt some companies will use the Act's provisions to raise money and then go bust within 18 months. There are going to be investors who find out they were not properly treated or were misled and then can't get their money out, and so on. Even with the best regime in place these things are a reality. That's why he was reassured that the system had an ongoing enforcement regime with the SEC and other tools in place such as the ability for private parties to bring lawsuits and seek redress accordingly.

In America we have one of the most robust capital markets in the world. This is in part because we have a private marketplace where people who are harmed can recover from that harm. It's one of the fundamental checks and balances that keep our economy on the straight and narrow. Title III crowdfunding was supposed to be a small experiment within a larger scope. When things go south, Andy thinks there's a lot of other stuff that's going to go south a lot faster and on a much bigger scale, and he hopes he designed Regulation CF in a way that folk have some sense of what they are getting into.

7

The White House: Doug Rand

Doug Rand's story at the White House began in September 2010. Despite being very much a political neophyte, he found himself in the extraordinarily fortuitous circumstance of showing up for his first day of work at the President Barack Obama's White House. For Doug, it was a dream come true. His path to getting there had been very serendipitous. He had never had a policy job before and had come to it as a public interest fellow newly graduated from law and business school. He had been a relatively older (30) law and business student, having spent most of his 20s building up a company in New York with his brother.

Doug was interested in entrepreneurship and was increasingly interested in policy. He was curious about how entrepreneurship could be encouraged through policy; this had been the subject of his fellowship project. It had led him to his position at the White House, working at the Office of Science and Technology Policy (OSTP). The OSTP is one of many different policy councils that work on just about everything you can think of. It was established in 1976, with a broad mandate to advise the president on the effects of science and technology on domestic and international affairs. At the time Doug came to the White House, new data suggested that there was something special and distinct about high-growth-potential companies: companies that were new and small today, but could rapidly grow and become large employers down the road. Doug's brief was to investigate this area as, at the time in 2010, the country was still relatively early in its recovery from the Great Recession and jobs, as a consequence, were on everybody's mind.

When he walked into work on his first day, it was just a couple of months before the 2010 midterm elections and most of the people around him had a pretty decent sense that things were not going to go so well. Likely, the prior two years of unified Democratic control of the Senate, the House, and the executive branch were probably coming to an end. Many in the building expected that the recent flurry of legislative activity was likely to become history. They were shifting their focus toward thinking, primarily, about making change through executive actions and private sector partners and using other tools in the toolkit that doesn't involve Congress. There was kind of a pre-gloom descending that Doug was only vaguely aware of at the time.

The White House that you are probably imagining right now is the building, the home, the iconic mansion. But very little work actually goes on there and, in fact, only one person actually has an office in the mansion and that's the president. It is his private office where he primarily works after hours.

The Oval Office that everybody is familiar with is actually not in the mansion. It's off to the side in the West Wing, which is not part of the residence. Indeed, it is a disproportionately small building in which so much important work gets done. It is where all the senior advisers work and that's where the president's daytime office is. The Oval. Across the street from that is a giant building called the Eisenhower Executive Office Building, which is where a thousand or two people work—people who are technically working for the White House. This was the building where Doug was stationed. These folk in these buildings, outside the West Wing, are among those who work directly on implementing the president's priorities.

There are many components within the White House—technically called the Executive Office of the President. Most of the people who work for the federal government don't work for the White House; they work for the Department of Veterans Affairs or the National Institutes of Health or the Department of Defense or any of the federal agencies everyone has come to know. These agencies include the 2-million-plus civilian federal employees who also work for the government and who consume the vast majority of taxpayer dollars. So, relatively speaking, the White House is a pretty small organization, but it's certainly larger than the impression given by *The West Wing* TV series.

The White House can be thought of as being divided into different functions. There's the press team—the communications team that does all the messaging to the press. There's the Office of the White House Counsel, which is where all the lawyers are. There are all these functional units that, to the outside world, appear to be part of the organization, but, for policy, there's a bunch of different offices that are responsible for different parts of formulating and executing the president's policy priorities. These include offices like the National Security Council, which owns all foreign policy and foreign aid; the National Economic Council; which is primarily responsible for domestic economic policy; and the Domestic Policy Council, whose pretty broad portfolio includes immigration, education, and healthcare policy. Basically, anything that isn't obviously economic policy falls under the remit of the Domestic Policy Council.

The OSTP, when Doug worked there, was a similar kind of department that, as can be imagined from the name, focused on science and technology. Inside this department there were people who worked on environmental policy and on hard science. It employed a ton of people who were PhD physicists, chemists, and biologists. Others worked on some nitty gritty science policy like how we should be spending taxpayer dollars to advance various scientific priorities at the agencies that fund research throughout the country. There was a new office that President Obama created within the OSTP for the newly created position of Chief Technology Officer, who worked on things like digital government and who looked at ways of applying technology to make the government work better.

Linking the OSTP to the JOBS Act and the story of the JOBS Act is, in some ways, a completely extraordinary story for which it's hard to draw grand principles of lawmaking. For Doug it was a wild ride because it happened during a time when nobody expected much in the way of legislation to be coming out of Congress. The Republicans had recently taken the House and were pretty reluctant to provide President Obama with any legislative victories. It looked like it was going to be gridlock for quite a while.

Yet the JOBS Act went from a line in a presidential speech to a Rose Garden signing ceremony in well under a year. Even in normal times that is supersonic speed for a policy idea to become law. Most people spend years and years grinding away at an idea before it gets introduced in Congress. And they keep plugging away, year after year after year, until finally there's a window of opportunity.

The story of the JOBS Act started in September 2011. It was just a little less than a year after Republicans had taken over the House of Representatives. They were well past the big-ticket legislative accomplishments of the first two years of Obama administration, where there had been the stimulus and the healthcare reform and Dodd Frank and other impactful triumphs. And now nothing significant was happening in Congress anymore because there was divided rule.

President Obama convened a joint session of Congress, which was unusual for any president to do. Obviously, the president addresses a joint session every January for the State of the Union address, but this was September and he convened Congress because he wanted to roll out a very large, very detailed legislative proposal which he called the American Jobs Act. This was the "American Jobs Act" in which the word "jobs" doesn't stand for anything—it's not an acronym. It just meant "jobs."

The Act included all kinds of proposals to try to rev up the economy and to accelerate the recovery from the Great Recession. Things like infrastructure investment and tax changes and changes to how unemployment insurance works. It was really a kitchen-sink set of proposals and the National Economic Council had a pretty critical role in formulating the ideas in the proposed Act.

So here was this gigantic legislative proposal that President Obama put forward in a joint session in which he gave a speech about what was in it and why it was important to make investments to accelerate job growth—a still urgent need for the country. He laid out all these different pieces of legislation which, if it had been passed verbatim, would in many ways have been a second stimulus.

The Act called for big investments that would have required a nontrivial amount of money. Not too many Republicans were psyched about making new investments and they weren't psyched about the original stimulus either—despite all the good that did. But a curious thing happened. There was one line in the president's speech where he said "we're also planning to cut away the red tape that prevents too many rapidly growing startup companies from raising capital and going public."

As with any State of the Union speech there was a lot of policy development that went into that line. To understand what that means one would go to the factsheet—a really long, detailed press release that the White House press office always puts out around the time of a presidential speech. It's a bit like double-clicking on the line on the speech and understanding the details of the policy thinking behind it. Anybody who was watching closely at home or as a member of Congress would be able to find out exactly what this meant.

What lay behind this particular line was that the administration wanted to work with the SEC to conduct a comprehensive review of securities regulations to reduce regulatory burdens on small business capital formation in ways that were consistent with investor protection.

And here's the key phrase: "including expanding crowdfunding opportunities and increasing mini-offerings." That was the first official signal that the White House was interested in doing something innovative in terms of securities regulations that would impact small startups and small businesses.

By the time of the president's speech, Congress had already been creating various capital formation bills. Things were floating around. Congressman Patrick McHenry had already authored one of the earlier crowdfunding bills. The original crowdfunding bill was inspired by some people who were trying to buy Pabst Blue Ribbon and who had been frustrated by what they saw as restrictive securities laws. In addition to McHenry, other Republican congressmen had been toying with some ideas around Regulation A, the mini public offerings, but nothing at the time of the president's speech had really gained any kind of traction yet.

In fact, Congress is full of bills that are introduced that never go anywhere even in the best of times. The capital formation bills, true to the way Congress works, were just ideas at the time that were in the ether. Of course, the White House can't take full credit for coming up with the genesis of the JOBS Act ideas from scratch, but when a democratic president includes something in a speech, something that Republicans are interested in, with a legislative proposal that is designed to appeal to Republicans, it was impactful and they took notice.

Indeed, the entire point of the American Jobs Act Proposal was that every single idea contained in it was something that had garnered bipartisan support in the past. The idea was to package a bunch of ideas to keep the economy growing. It was at a time when the country desperately needed new ideas, and every single one of the ideas outlined by the president had been endorsed by Republicans at some point in the past: So why not pass it all right now?

A politically potent argument but sadly not a winning argument. There were many components of the American Jobs Act that were ultimately passed in different ways in the year to come without the branding of one giant bipartisan bill.

At the time of the speech every word had been heavily vetted and a ton of thought from a ton of people had gone into it. ("The good ol' days," reminisces Doug, nostalgically.) To understand where the JOBS Act came from, one has to go back a little bit further—to around the time when Doug started at the White House—which was almost a year before the speech was made. Doug recalls a series of remarkable events. He had a new boss and mentor named Tom Kalil who was second-in-command of the OSTP. He also was an adviser for the National Economic Council. Tom had a foot in both worlds—economic policy on the one hand and science and tech on the other. He was an eight-year Clinton administration veteran and he ended up doing all eight years for the Obama administration. Doug describes him as being an unsung hero of technology innovation in this country. Tom had a vision and he charged lots of people with different parts of that vision.

Doug's slice of that was to go out and find some of the best ideas that people had for improving the climate for high-growth entrepreneurship in communities across the country. Not just in technology but in all different kinds of industries because, knowing entrepreneurship as Doug did, he recognized that great entrepreneurs can and do come from anywhere; they're disproportionately responsible for job creation and are disproportionately responsible for innovation. Doug felt that, critically, even professional investors don't know, by and large, what the successful startups are going to be beforehand.

In fact, Doug knew that even the most successful investors probably only hit a home run one time out of one hundred. He understood that as a representative of the government he shouldn't be picking winners but should just be figuring out a way to improve the climate, overall. He set about reading papers and policy proposals, and talking to lots of people in trying to understand what the government should be prioritizing when, during his first week on the job, Tom sent him an e-mail.

It was a very short e-mail that said something along the lines of "You know, you should really look into this idea of crowdfunding" and Doug thought to himself, "OK first I need to figure out what Crowdfunding is." Remember, this was at a time when Kickstarter and other similar platforms were just barely entering the public consciousness.

Most of the popular crowdfunding platforms that people know and love today either didn't exist or were just getting off the ground. That was one of the reasons he got in touch with Jenny Kassan and a number of other people who were the early thinkers on the idea of "what crowdfunding is" and what were the trends that they were seeing at the time.

What he started to hear was that while the industry at the time was all donation based, what if it could be equity based and what would that mean for capital formation? Why haven't these policies changed in several generations? What would the risk to investors be if things did change significantly? How could that risk be mitigated in a responsible way?

Doug understood that answering questions like these was how a lot of policies get developed. Doubtless other people were having similar conversations. It takes a lot of hard work on the part of policy people, not just at the White House but in federal agencies and by staffs of various members of Congress, to get something done.

But for Doug it was a really interesting journey from the moment he started through the next couple of years. A fascinating education about what ideas were out there on capital formation and in understanding how and whether something like crowdfunding could be applied to a more modern regulatory scheme for the completely different world of securities.

While there is no standard way that ideas emerge into policies and then ultimately into laws, Doug describes an abbreviated version of the causal chain of how the JOBS Act came to be. The American Jobs Act speech triggered everything and was a pivotal moment in the life of what became the JOBS Act, the acronym, because that was when the idea of crowdfunding first had presidential endorsement. And getting presidential endorsement doesn't happen every day.

From that moment, after the speech, things really started to snowball. What were several ideas that had been floating around still needed to get fleshed out. At the time, there was an independent council of CEOs and other business leaders who recommend job creation policies to the president, and they had just issued a report. It included infrastructure investment and tax changes and a bunch of other ideas, but it also had some very specific proposals on capital formation.

They recommended changing Sarbanes-Oxley for public companies. They recommended some changes to seed funding. And they had this line saying "We propose that small investors be allowed to use crowdfunding." Shortly following the president's jobs council endorsement of the idea, an independent, self-appointed task force that had been in conversation with the Treasury Department presented its final report proposing something called the "IPO on-ramp."

The on-ramp is the part of the JOBS Act that made a big difference in the public securities markets and it was the first official publication of the idea. The idea came from outside of government: the idea being that instead of exempting companies from Sarbanes-Oxley, how about giving them just a little bit more time before they matured into full compliance with Sarbanes-Oxley? It was an interesting idea that gained traction almost immediately.

Then in November 2011, Congressman Patrick McHenry (R-North Carolina) got a vote on his crowdfunding bill, which, at the time, was the only crowdfunding bill. The Obama administration endorsed it even though it was authored by Republicans and even though it didn't necessarily look like what the administration would have wanted the final thing to look like. But it was a good start and so, in some carefully calibrated language, the White House put out an official endorsement of this Republican bill. It passed with a lot of bipartisan support: 407 votes to 17.

Another turning point was in January 2012. The administration hadn't publicly released a lot of details about what it would like to see in a final crowdfunding bill that the president would actually sign, let alone a final IPO on-ramp bill or a mini public offering. The ideas were put out there in a very abbreviated form and so there was a question about what the president would actually sign.

January 31, 2012, was the one-year anniversary of the Startup America initiative that Doug had helped launch. He had worked on bringing all of the federal agencies and a bunch of private sector players together to drive a new agenda to promote high-growth entrepreneurship, but hadn't really involved formal legislation at that point. To reiterate, it was post-midterm, so everyone was really focused on executive action and private public partnerships. But a few weeks earlier, at year end, there was interest from the Hill from both parties in some of these capital formation ideas. In response, the White House released something called the Startup America Legislative Agenda, which proposed a lot of things. It proposed some tax changes; it proposed one small immigration change that would have been really favorable for entrepreneurs and high-skilled folk.

But the meat of it was fleshing out three proposed changes to the securities laws. One of them was in expanding offerings eligible under Regulation A. One of them was creating a national framework for equity-based crowdfunding and one of them was creating the IPO on-ramp. Importantly, this agenda went into a lot more detail about what the White House would like to see in any bill that the president would sign.

And the reason it was important that the president signal support for these ideas was that ultimately no matter what happens in the House and Senate, the president needs to sign it into law eventually. Since he was endorsing it, everyone understood that if they put the effort in, it could actually become law. That being said, before a bill reaches the president's desk there are countless hurdles: for example, does anyone on the relevant committee actually care and want it to see the light of day? And this is not just in the Senate but in the House too; the question is, do the leaders of both parties in both chambers actually care and want to get a vote? Or do they have other priorities? A lot of the time even seeing an open door of presidential endorsement at the end of the road doesn't matter because Congress is split between two parties and one party is dead set against that thing ever happening.

Indeed, to fully appreciate what an achievement it was that the JOBS Act made it through the legislative gauntlet, it is worth keeping in mind that 99.9 percent of the bills that are introduced in Congress in any given year never reach a vote. And fear of a presidential veto is the very last barrier.

In the case of the JOBS Act what was kind of interesting and very special was the fact that it changed securities regulations and was, essentially, deregulatory. Republicans like things that are deregulatory. Furthermore, it was a regulatory change that was not an appropriation—it didn't cost anything. Republicans are in general more willing to consider something that's not going to involve public spending—at least public spending of the kind they don't typically endorse. In this way, it was unusual. Here was a Democratic president endorsing some pretty forward-leaning ideas that were both deregulatory and didn't cost anything, and everyone wanted to bask in the glow of job creation and assistance for small business.

Consequently, the ideas were taken relatively seriously by members of both parties in both chambers of Congress because, while it's never a good idea to bet that legislation is actually going to make it through that gauntlet, in this case it seemed like something that might actually make it.

Everyone in Congress really stepped on the gas after the Startup America Legislative Agenda was announced because now there was a tangible framework that one could either agree with or disagree with. But there it was. It was something to start writing bills around and was a starting point for negotiation.

Then one day Doug Rand woke up and saw that Eric Cantor was holding a press conference to announce the creation of a new piece of legislation that he was calling the JOBS Act. Cantor named it. He or someone in his office came up with the acronym for Jumpstart Our Business Startups. The JOBS Act.

And that was the moment Doug realized that if Eric Cantor was going to stick the epithet "JOBS Act" on a piece of legislation when all anyone cares about was jobs, he must be serious. What Cantor had done was to take the crowdfunding bill that had already passed Congress and stapled a bunch of things to it, including the mini public offering along with a version of the IPO on-ramp and a couple of other things that the White House had never formally endorsed, and said, "OK here it is! We're calling it the JOBS Act," and he brought it up for a vote.

The White House provided a qualified endorsement saying the administration supported passing the bill with the expectation that more kinks would be worked out in the Senate. And with that endorsement the thing passed overwhelmingly in a bipartisan way: 390 votes to 23.

After the bill had passed the House it went over to the Senate, where there was an intense flurry of activity. Democrats and Republicans and their staff did what the Senate does—make modifications to conform it to the senator's ideas of what it should be. That process was pretty intense. In the end, the McHenry version of the crowdfunding bill got excised and replaced with a new piece of legislation that was co-authored by Senators Merkley and Michael Bennet (D-Colorado) on the Democratic side and Senator Scott Brown (R-Massachusetts) on the Republican side, which was much more in line with President Obama's original proposal.

That all got a vote in the Senate rather than going to a conference committee. A conference committee is one in which the House and Senate versions are laboriously harmonized. The House just went ahead and passed the Senate version and it went to the president's desk. And that's how this signing ceremony in April 2012 came about and is the short version of how you get from Congress to Rose Garden in well under a year—which is crazy fast.

The Lobbyists

Every bill has constituents with vested interests who want to see policy adopted. Most of the time these constituents are represented by professional lobbyists. Focusing just on the crowdfunding piece and not the public equities part, Doug recalls that, remarkably, there were no big crowdfunding lobbies in any form that anyone would recognize. There were no K Street fat cats lobbying for crowdfunding, trying to knock down the doors of the White House, charging hundreds of dollars an hour to set up meetings for their clients.

It was a true grassroots idea and it just happened to be in the right place at the right time. And it happened to have some advocates who worked really hard to seize the opportunities that had fallen in their lap. To be clear, there were plenty of people in the executive and legislative branches who had longstanding interests in crowdfunding. Doug first began figuring out who was smart on these issues by talking to law professors who specialize in securities law. He spoke to anyone who had written anything about crowdfunding. He says that there was something in the water when they launched the Startup

America initiative in January 2011, when he was barnstorming the country, holding roundtables in various cities where he asked people for their ideas of what the administration might do to help small business startups.

And crowdfunding came up. A lot.

There was a growing awareness that if you can raise money on Kickstarter without offering any hope of a return on investment by calling it a donation, then there should be a way to do the same for small companies without triggering this regulatory regime designed for giant public companies. Different people had become frustrated by the status quo and saw an opportunity in crowdfunding. Companies were already starting to use Kickstarter for crowdfunding, the Pebble Technology Corporation, for example. But every entrepreneur who was looking at crowdfunding was asking: *Why can't I offer a return on investment?* It came up a lot.

Doug also came across Woodie Neiss, who was an entrepreneur in Florida. Woodie had been successful with his own company at the time and, not knowing any better, had thought that he would like to sell shares in his company to his customers because they were his biggest fans. He wanted to offer them the opportunity to share the upside. Naturally, his lawyers had told him that he absolutely couldn't do that. As is common, being told by a lawyer that you can't do something makes people consider alternatives. Woodie just couldn't shake the idea.

It didn't seem right that he couldn't do it and, unlike most people, he became obsessed with this snag in the securities regulations that prevented him from crowdfunding his company. Woodie, in cooperation with a number of other people, wrote some ideas about what crowdfunding should look like and they started gathering signatures. It was out there on the Internet for anyone to see and it had clearly been written by someone who had done a fair amount of thinking about this and who had been living it. It resonated with Doug Rand.

He called Woodie and started talking to him about it. Doug immediately realized that here was a guy who was in the right place at the right time. What impressed Doug was that Woodie didn't just say, "OK I've written a position paper and I'm done with it." In 2011 these ideas were starting to gain traction. On his own dime, along with some allies, Woodie started coming to Washington and buttonholing congressional staffers trying to do everything they could to help people understand why this was a good idea, and to help explain how some of the risks could be mitigated.

Doug saw that they had a passion project and thought that was just a wonderful example of somebody having an idea that they really thought was good and right. People who were willing to put in the blood, sweat and tears of educating actual policymakers about how it all might work.

Woodie's focus was on small businesses, which was consistent with Doug's brief. At no time were any real estate companies, individuals, or lobbyists knocking on Doug's door. The JOBS Act was intended to create jobs primarily through operating companies and through entrepreneurs growing startups that would employ a lot of people—making it easier for them to access capital. Revolutionizing capital formation for and access to real estate deals just wasn't the official thrust of what anyone was trying to do.

That being said, Doug knew that they were innovating within a regulatory framework that was all about private placements and private capital formation and that, obviously, real estate was a big part of that and always had been. He was mindful of the fact that any of the changes he was working on would probably have some unintended consequences. He was mostly concerned, though, with negative unintended consequences and investor protection. Doug thinks that to the extent that real estate investment has been democratized and, presuming that people are not being reckless about it, maybe it's a positive unintended consequence. But at no time was it ever an "expected" unintended consequence and it was never a primary intended consequence.

Doug was familiar with policy ideas being pushed really hard by organizations with strong vested interests. He most often saw this with tax cut legislation lobbyists, who would swarm Washington when a particular policy was going to boost, literally, the bottom line of their clients. More often than not, a bunch of special interest groups push for something that benefits them marginally. Fortunately, that's not always the way it works, and the JOBS Act was a nice example of everyone being open to new ideas. Folk like Doug were proactive in pounding the pavement for insights from unlikely places. They still had to be thoroughly vetted of course; they weren't just going to be copied and pasted from some advocate's brain onto a piece of legislation. But Doug heard good ideas percolating up from all kinds of places and he integrated these into the support coming from the White House.

Event Planning

The Act passed the Senate, re-passed the House, and then went to the president to sign. At that point everyone knew that the president was going to sign it, so Doug and his team shifted from the realm of serious negotiations and policymaking to the world of event planning. They figured they'd put together a nice ceremony to sign the bipartisan legislation. It was decided that the picturesque Rose Garden was an appropriate venue for the ceremony.

It turned out to be a really beautiful day. Doug wanted to make sure that as many people as possible who had some part in coming up with the ideas in the JOBS Act were invited to the Rose Garden. Among the many, he invited Woodie Neiss and Jenny Kassan, another independent lobbyist.

He went through all of his old e-mails, double and triple checking to make sure he was really honoring all the people who had a hand in this success. He made sure that the invitees went beyond the obvious Congressional members. Several of them wanted to stand behind the president and smile while he signed the bill. That's all for the best, but Doug wanted to be sure that a bill that was empowering every member of "the crowd" also honored those from the crowd outside of government who had played a role in making the whole thing happen.

Concerns

Doug has always hoped that the investor protections would hold in a meaningful way. He also hoped that this would not just be remembered as that bill that lets you get in on the ground floor of the next Facebook. Some people outside of government were thinking and licking their chops at the very thought.

He hoped that this would be a way for entrepreneurs, in particular, to access capital because he felt it was too easy to ignore entrepreneurs who are not as well connected to the traditional sources of capital. He wanted to ensure that they were able to tap their customers and their communities and be able to get off the ground in greater numbers and prosper in greater numbers. He often found himself talking about crowdfunding as the twenty-first-century version of barn raising, where a community comes together to build something important.

Understanding how extraordinary the impact has been on real estate, Doug thinks that, on the one hand, you can say this is a great thing because it's allowing investors to get a better return. That's great if that's happening as long as relatively unsophisticated folk aren't losing their shirts. On the other hand, he wonders if it is enabling real estate projects in communities that really need it or if it is stimulating the kinds of housing developments that are in short supply. Is it engendering more socially impactful real estate development that might not otherwise happen? Doug, for one, certainly hopes it might.

8

Rich Uncles: Harold Hofer

Harold Hofer is Canadian born and a subject of the Queen, like the author. He moved to California when he was a kid and grew up in the Los Angeles area, eventually attending the University of California Los Angeles, where he received both undergraduate and master's degrees in economics and then went on to get a law degree. After working in a law firm for a couple of years, Harold's former college roommate, who was then working for a real estate firm in Orange County, suggested they go into business together, assembling syndications for the projects his firm was building and selling.

They started by using Regulation D private placement partnerships to buy real estate during the 1980s, raising approximately $80 million in equity for some $300 million worth of real estate. In the mid-1990s they sold their company to Koll in Newport Beach, California, run at the time by Ray Wirta, Harold's current partner. In 1997 Ray merged Koll with the predecessor to CBRE and ascended to the CEO role, where he had a successful ride, later taking the company private and then public again.

Ray retired as active CEO of CBRE in 2005 and assumed the role of executive chairman. Now that he was retired, he could revisit the other things he had always wanted to accomplish but hadn't been able to because of his position within CBRE. One thing on the list was finding a way to use the Internet to aggregate investor capital to buy real estate. Harold and Ray noticed that the real estate industry was slow to embrace modern technologies during a time when other industries and companies were already effectively using the Internet to create efficiencies and cost savings. They saw an opportunity to use the Internet to raise capital online for real estate investment rather than through broker dealers, as was commonplace at the time.

In 2006 they put together a public offering, aiming to raise $3 million from small investors by offering ownership interests in a shopping center they had acquired in Texas, setting the minimum investment at $2500.

They advertised in different ways in an attempt to interest people. They put flyers on the door knobs of homes around the shopping center they had purchased. They even put a sign out on the street that said, "Own a piece of the shopping center; go to the website!"

Yet, despite these efforts, they didn't gain much traction. Harold wondered if they weren't, perhaps, ahead of their time in terms of market receptivity to this new idea. Plus, the economy went off the edge of the cliff shortly after they started, not a trivial thing, which dramatically reduced interest from potential investors. The idea was the right one, but at the wrong time, so they mothballed the effort even though they had no intention of giving it up completely.

Harold remained intrigued with the idea of aggregating small investors' capital online to buy real estate and, since one of the premises of the 2012 JOBS Act was to make the aggregation of capital easier for small businesses, he saw an opportunity to resurrect their idea. The JOBS Act jarred his and Ray's thinking. They realized the market was pulling out of recession and that the Act would result in people jumping on the bandwagon to raise capital for real estate investing from a whole disparate group of investors with an online platform, and that they should too. They wanted to expose offering opportunities to smaller, non-accredited investors.

It was well known that the JOBS Act allowed many different permutations, but the primary initial thing that intrigued Harold and Ray was that it allowed for general solicitation. In Texas they had been restricted to advertising in only that state, but the new regulations allowed for advertising nationwide. Their premise had always been to open offerings to nonmillionaire, non-accredited investors, so what was particularly interesting about the JOBS Act was that it introduced Regulation A+. Regulation A+ allowed for offerings of up to $50 million and, importantly, for general solicitation of both accredited and non-accredited investors alike.

Harold and Ray were cautious though and, not certain how the new rules would be tested by regulators, chose not to avail themselves initially of the Regulation A+ solution in pursuing their idea of bringing real estate to nonmillionaire investors. Instead, they opted to do another intrastate public offering, this time in California. Launching in 2013, they used the REIT structure they were familiar with from their work in Texas six years earlier. Restricted to selling only to California residents, they identified website visitor locations via the IP addresses used when accessing the platform. This allowed them to preclude access to the platform if someone was trying to invest from anywhere other than California.

The initial plan was for a $25 million equity offering with a minimum investment of $500. Investor demand was so high that they had to upsize the fund twice from $25 to $50 million, and then again to $100 million. They quickly realized that people want to own real estate and, given an easy way to access it, will become active investors.

Nontraded real estate investment trusts (REITs) had been selling to these kinds of retail investors for many years through broker dealers, but with a 10 percent commission associated with it. Harold and Ray's business model went directly to the consumer via the Internet and presented the same investment opportunity, thereby eliminating the 10 percent commission. Their thought was not to necessarily disintermediate the broker dealer community by transacting online, but rather to expose the sort of investment opportunity to investors who qualified for the offering financially but did not have a broker.

When they started in California, it was initially just Harold and Ray. They had a portfolio of Del Taco investments they already owned that they used to seed the California REIT. At first, they exposed it to family and friends, and then they put together a rudimentary website. In late 2013 Harold reconnected with Howard Makler. Howard was a marketing guy and Harold had known him for as long as he'd known Ray. He came from the real estate shopping center business just like Harold, and he brought a marketing expertise to the team that Harold and Ray did not have. Howard created the Rich Uncles veneer for the platform and figured out how to get people to the site and how to make the site interesting enough to encourage people to invest.

By late 2014, Harold and Howard had rented an executive suite and were trying to figure out how to get this new entity from A to B. As the company grew, they layered on additional staff in four disciplines: real estate, their core competency; tech; finance and accounting; and investor relations.

As they were not broker dealers they couldn't cold call people, trying to get them to invest in the platform, but they did put in place a staff that responded to inquiries from people interested in the platform. Their growth was slow, deliberate, and organic. They never raised money from a venture capital firm, although they talked to several and received term sheets. Instead they preferred to raise growth capital from friends and family.

From the onset, the biggest challenge for Harold's model was customer acquisition. How do you find the customer who actually wants to invest in real estate? How do you create a web platform and get people to your website to begin with? And once they are there, how do you create a compelling enough story to want them to make an investment decision?

Historically, this product type was sold through financial planners and broker dealers, who earned a commission to put the client into the product. The broker told a story, explaining the product on behalf of the capital-raising client. Now, the challenge was to create an opportunity when there was no storyteller: one in which the investor has to be nurtured through the decision-making process online.

That was, and remains, the biggest challenge: how to make the website known to people so they'll come to the site, and, once there, how to create a compelling enough story that they'll want to make an investment. To meet this challenge, Harold and his team kept the size of the minimum investment at the same $500 as they had in the first California REIT and launched a national REIT that was also a net lease product. For a subsequent national Regulation A+ student housing REIT, Harold reduced the minimum to an industry record at the time of only $5, thinking that reducing the investment decision barrier to such a low figure might make people think, *What the heck, why not give it a shot!*

To drive web traffic, digital ads and pay per click on Google and Facebook have been a successful advertising media. Now, tens of thousands of people have registered on the site, so e-mail campaigns go out not only to the existing base of investors but also to many other people who expressed enough interest in the platform to register. This helps move the needle along and make more people aware of offerings.

Rich Uncles ultimately converts about one in three people who register on its site. This is a very high conversion rate, but the challenge remains in getting people to the website and, once registered there, to create a smooth enough journey that they will make investment decisions. By having a low $5 entry point it becomes a no-brainer to make a small investment and see how things work out; the hope is that investors eventually elect to make a more material investment.

The initial offering in California closed in the middle of 2016. Even though the ramp-up was slow, it gradually accelerated and they raised over $85 million. Since it played out so well in California, they started investigating how the process could be rolled out nationally. JOBS Act regulations allowed for national solicitation using a REIT structure within a Regulation A+ Tier 2 format, but this new legislation had a $50 million cap on how much they could raise within 12 months.

Harold was aware that some platforms were using Regulation A+ to raise more than $50 million in any given year by creating entities that specialized in different asset classes or geographical regions and simultaneously issuing independent Regulation A+ offerings in each of those classes and regions. It was possible, Harold thought, especially so soon after the rules had been promulgated that the SEC would see these simultaneous offerings as one, and integrate them, concluding that users were simply trying to evade the intent of the Act. Being uncertain how that might eventually play out, Harold and Ray were leery of being the guinea pig trying to test that system.

With this concern in mind, and although Regulation A+ was a far simpler solution, Harold and Ray didn't want to be limited by size, so they opted instead to do an S-11 fully registered offering through the SEC, of a non-traded public REIT which had no upper limit in scale.

The whole premise of the Rich Uncles platform Harold and Ray founded is different from most other crowdfunding platforms. Whereas other platforms try to create a marketplace matching accredited investors with real estate sponsors, Rich Uncles' business model has always been to make the product available to non-accredited investors. Plus, importantly, they are the actual end-user of the capital they raise and not just a matchmaking site. Harold and Ray are real estate people by background, not tech people, so rather than taking investor money and giving it to a third-party real estate sponsor, they thought they could do just as good a job, or better, by investing in capital directly.

As principals they already had their own deal flow, so their initial challenge was in finding investors. Their business model differed from that of their peers in two important ways. First, they were aggregating capital from non-accredited investors, whereas, initially, nearly all the other platforms focused on accredited investors. And secondly, they were the principals in their own deals rather than working with other sponsors. A couple of platforms have since morphed to embrace non-accredited investors, but Rich Uncles was among the earliest pioneers of this model.

They started with two products. The first was a single-tenant, triple net lease product. They reasoned that, looking at a spectrum of real estate through the lens of relative risk returns, perhaps the riskiest asset class is hospitality, since the income stream can change daily depending on occupancy and room rates. On the other side of the spectrum are the single-tenant net lease product types: long-term leases with creditworthy tenants on a triple net basis, meaning tenants pay all property taxes, insurance, and maintenance. Being one of the lower risk asset classes, Rich Uncles focused on the single-tenant, triple net lease properties.

To further reduce risk, they chose to keep leverage, the amount borrowed against a property, at a conservative 50 percent limit. By starting with an investment product type with low risk and low leverage, they were able to create a story that was easily understandable to a novice real estate investor who may have previously had very limited exposure to real estate investing.

They also thought that the triple net lease product would be easy to explain to novice investors because it is a straightforward current passive income product with simple percentage returns similar to interest in fixed-income instruments, something familiar to everyone. Harold thought if they tried to explain what the "internal rate of return" means, their investors' eyes would likely glaze over. So keeping the product type based on something similar to interest on a bank deposit kept it simple and easy to understand.

Since inception, Rich Uncles has continually sought ways of further simplifying offerings to non-accredited investors. Looking at the broader landscape of 260 million adults in the United States, only 11 million or so are accredited investors. Adding investors to that pool who qualify for Rich Uncles' single-tenant net lease offering, that is, those with $75,000 in income per year or $250,000 of net worth, the available population goes up by another 25 million people.

This represents about the top 15 percent of the US adult population. The intriguing thing about the JOBS Act Regulation A+ option is that it effectively opens real estate investing to everyone. The only limitation with Regulation A+ Tier 2 is that investors must represent that the investment they make does not exceed 10 percent of their annual income or 10 percent of their net worth. This levels the playing field entirely, so Rich Uncles decided to launch a Regulation A+ offering to invest in student housing deals, which is the product they used to offer the $5 minimum investment.

Having a minimum so low, Rich Uncles' idea is to make it easy for anybody to dip a toe into the real estate investing waters. In the initial years, the typical investor Rich Uncles attracted to the triple net lease product had an average age of 48, with about 40 percent of the investment money raised from retirement accounts. The business was successful; they were raising money and buying real estate every month, but couldn't get the contagion they were looking for. Recognizing that a younger generation would likely be more comfortable with investing online, Rich Uncles decided to shift their focus to millennial audiences using a $5 minimum as the entry point for investors. The broader investment thesis for the student housing product is not just that it is a yield play but also that it has a small potential value-added component in that rental streams tend to adjust annually as new students move into the facility.

Student housing has evolved very rapidly over the last ten years or so. Before then, it was either on-campus housing or some apartment near campus with a bunch of students crammed into a room. Purpose-built student housing only started to emerge in the early 2000s and is a product class where developers build properties geared specifically to students. These properties might have four or five bedrooms located around a common area that includes a kitchen, living room, and laundry area. Students either share a bathroom or have their own. This housing is built with students in mind from the ground up, rather than trying to retrofit an existing apartment building to accommodate them. It is proving to be a very robust and vibrant community business model.

The economics are similar to multifamily deals, but the cap rates going in are a little higher than traditional multifamily. Rich Uncles thinks this is a similarly low-risk, entry-level investment suitable for online investors because if they are acquired and managed properly, occupancy levels should remain high during the course of the year and leases are typically guaranteed by parents. This type of investment fits in well with Rich Uncles' intent to create a second product type that is easy to understand.

A significant limitation of most crowdfunded real estate deals is that once an investment is made, there is no secondary market for the shares. In other words, investors cannot typically trade them on a market anywhere, or sell them to anyone. To ameliorate this issue, Rich Uncles chose to offer a buyback option. The national single-tenant net lease REIT has a share repurchase program where they will buy up to 20 percent of the outstanding shares per year annually from shareholders, which creates liquidity for investors.

The JOBS Act reawakened the initial premise for Harold and his partner Ray; they could sell a real estate investment product through an online platform to nonmillionaire investors. They were the first to try it way back in 2006, and even when the economy fell in 2007 and 2008, and all the way through the Great Recession, they continued to believe the idea was a good one. It has always been their business model and the JOBS Act allowed them to open the market for all investors. Most importantly, it allowed them to openly solicit investors nationwide. When the Act passed, Harold realized other people were going to be jumping into real estate crowdfunding also. He knew they would start putting together crowdfunding platforms, so, along with Ray, he decided to jump back in himself and focus exclusively on the non-accredited investor.

At the time they were dusting off their earlier 2005 idea when the JOBS Act passed, they were unaware that the likes of Fundrise, RealtyShares, RealtyMogul, and Patch of Land were creating marketplaces by pairing up accredited investors with real estate sponsors. But they did anticipate that the JOBS Act would give rise to companies who were also attempting to eliminate some of the barriers to raising capital for small businesses and that this would doubtless include real estate.

Long-Term JOBS Act Potential

Harold thinks it remains uncertain where the crowdfunding real estate industry is going to end up. He believes one of the main elements of the JOBS Act that was the most influential for real estate was in allowing general solicitation to investors. He thinks the jury is still out as to how viable that's going to be. Most of his competitors in the crowdfunding space have pursued the accredited investor channel and reached various levels of success, but nobody has really killed it yet with that strategy. The second major impact of the JOBS Act relates to the Regulation A+ investment concept. Harold wonders if it will catch fire with the likes of Fundrise using Regulation A+ or multiple Regulation A+ products on their platform. Will the Regulation A+ concept make it easy for real estate investment sponsors to raise capital? Or as Harold believes, is it still too early in the stage of that evolution to tell how viable it's going to be in the long term?

"The deciding factor," Harold says, "will be the degree to which the market embraces investing in real estate this way."

The reason he and his partners created a $5 product is to make it appealing to millennials. Harold's oldest child is a millennial, and she and her husband think of investing in an entirely different way than he would. Today, in contrast to when Harold was their age, everything is done online through an app. Understanding the implications of this is important in effectively molding the investment behavior of younger people as they think about investing in real estate.

Being able to go to an online platform like Rich Uncles to invest in real estate, as the younger investors of today can, was not an option Harold's generation ever had.

Harold thinks the future of real estate investing is going to migrate to the online world. He wonders if he can create contagion among the millennial set to mold their thinking about how to invest in real estate. Since the time he first tried to sell real estate to investors in Texas, years before the JOBS Act passed, he thought people wanted options other than just investing in a listed REIT or opening an account at a stock brokerage firm where a broker invested on their behalf. Harold hopes they opt instead to invest in real estate online through Rich Uncles, where he believes the future lies.

9

Fundrise: Ben Miller

Ben Miller filed a patent in February 2011 for an idea to market real estate on the Internet, fully a year before the JOBS Act was passed and before anyone in Congress had even begun thinking about such an idea. The idea came to Ben during a period when the United States and the world economy were in shambles. He thinks it's incredible the contrast in sentiment ten years later, where people are feeling sanguine compared to how they were feeling during the Great Recession of 2008. Within those ten years, unemployment had dropped from above 10 percent to a very low 4 percent—4 percent, being close to full employment. Ben equates the contrast to a comparison of the 1950s and the 1970s: two completely different eras.

Ten years after the Great Recession, everything seemed to be moving faster to Ben. When he conceived his idea in September 2010, it was right in the middle of this sort of post-financial crisis gloom. It was born out of a feeling that the system was broken and that it was unreliable and couldn't be trusted. The system wasn't dishonest, but one did not have faith that it was able to deliver. There is this inherent trust that you can turn on a faucet and water will come out. During the Great Recession, people simply lost faith in the global financial system.

Technology platforms were beginning to grow; people were beginning to get a sense that great change was happening. Social media was in its infancy; Living Social and Groupon were popular and Facebook was only 24 months old. There were lots of interesting things happening and Ben was looking at this world fraught with doubt on the one hand and optimism on the other. He thought that there had to be an alternative to what was not only a failing financial system, but a state that was on the verge of complete collapse.

At the time, Ben was buying small urban infill, historic buildings in Washington DC in emerging neighborhoods that were rundown and considered dangerous. Urban infill is defined as existing land which is mostly built-out; what is being built is in effect "filling in" the gaps. He was concentrating on finding deals in what had been the first retail district of Washington DC where companies like Sears Roebuck had built in the 1930s. Theirs and other buildings had been vacant since the 1960s and he was trying to buy and renovate these locations.

The people he knew in finance were not interested in providing capital because they thought that the locations were too urban. Between 1950 and 2000, the trend had been development in suburban locations; Ben's ideas were ahead of their time. That combined with an environment where the financial institutions were essentially in tatters—a setting that provided little interest in growth—Ben found it difficult to raise money for his projects.

Something changed in September 2010. Ben was in contract to buy an entire city block in Washington DC for a very good price. Neighborhood residents expressed encouragement about the site that would include homes and restaurants. The neighbors were enthusiastic; the financial institutions were remote, dispassionate, and essentially uninvested emotionally in its potential. Ben recognized the tremendous disconnect. The lightbulb came on—why not go to the people who were so excited about the project for the capital he needed?

It seems like a no-brainer now—people are interested in the betterment of their own neighborhoods. Not just in DC—but everywhere. So why not replicate the process throughout the country? But there was a problem—a lot of people were distrustful about putting their money back into a system that had all but failed. People, he reasoned, were thinking that while they didn't trust the system, they were interested in investing in growth. One neighborhood at a time. People wanted to rebuild the country.

He remembers going to a Silicon Valley friend who was in the tech business and asking how he could bring real estate to the people from a practical, online perspective. His friend told him that he would need a half-dozen security people and database people and front-end engineers and Ben, with no tech background, didn't understand any of it. Frustrated with this he asked one of his soccer buddies, a software developer, what he knew about all of this. It turned out this soccer friend was to be the best software developer Ben would ever meet. To this day, Ben says that he is the most incredibly talented person in the field of software development.

The guy could do almost all the things that this Silicon Valley friend had outlined and, better than that, he could do almost all of it single-handedly. So in January 2011, together with Ben's brother, the three started working on a business plan. The hardest thing in the beginning was figuring out how they were going to do what they wanted to do. There were three key challenges: (1) they had to buy real estate, so they would have something practical to work on; (2) they had to build out a software platform, which meant building a website for something that had never been done before; and (3) they had to establish a legal mechanism which at the time didn't exist.

Ben was aware of no legal or regulatory structure for raising money for real estate investment over the Internet. Nothing existed for an equity investment in a company, let alone for investment in real estate. Ben called law firm after law firm and visited a dozen more, trying to figure out who could help him do it. Most ironically, in mid-2011, he went to a large law firm that was best known for representing investment banks. The meeting was held in their conference room, located in New York City's Times Square. Ben met with their heads of securities and real estate practices.

Ben remembers the meeting as if it were yesterday. He presented his idea; he described how he wanted to find new ways for developers to bring real estate deals to investors. He explained that this would require a reinvention of the existing system. And he asked if and how they could assist him in finding a way to do it, legally. At the end of his impassioned speech, Ben recalls clearly, one of the attorneys asked him, "You know," he said, "why would you want to bother with the little people?"

The idea of doing this was so novel that people thought Ben was just plain crazy. He had all but given up on the idea when sometime, in late 2011, by pure luck a friend of his retired from the SEC. The friend had been the head of Internet Enforcement for the SEC. Ben thought that this was exactly the guy he should ask. His friend told him of the one person in America who would know how to do what Ben wanted to do, and that's how Ben got introduced to Marty Dunn.

Marty was, and remains, a true guru of securities law in the United States. He had held increasingly senior positions at the SEC, culminating as general counsel and acting corporate finance director. Marty had written the original Regulation A and had just moved to the private sector. When he heard Ben's pitch his simple, encouraging response was "Oh, that sounds like fun. Let's do it!"

Their first filing with the SEC was in December 2011. Marty dusted off Regulation A, which hadn't been used much in real estate, having been largely superseded by Regulation D. He worked with it to allow for money to be raised on the Internet from the general public. Marty had this deep, nearly photographic memory of everything, and he knew everyone. He knew all the ins and outs and, together with Ben, spent time crafting a filing that they submitted to the SEC that shoehorned into some of their small business regulations.

Ben hears a lot of rhetoric about regulators being difficult to work with, but when he went to the SEC in 2011, there was a very real concern about small business capital formation. The SEC was interested in finding new, innovative ways to bring finance to these companies. When the two men went to the SEC with Ben's idea, staff at the organization thought they were crazy, but were willing to entertain them. Ben submitted his filing, providing six duplicate copies of copious documents. Total weight in paper—25 pounds.

For those interested in such things, here is the process. To conduct a public offering, which was the process Ben was effectively employing, there is a Form S-1 that has to be completed and submitted. For real estate companies the equivalent form is Form 11, and for a Regulation A submission there is a Form 1A, which no one was using at the time. With Marty's guidance, Ben had essentially rejiggered Form 1A to make it work to meet the need.

Ben remembers the first filing rejection: the SEC responded that the paperwork had not been completed properly. An organization issue, they said. Ben dutifully resubmitted the form which, by the way, ran more than 200 pages long.

Once submitted the SEC, by its own rules, had to respond within 30 days with questions, which they call "comments." The comment letter initiated a back and forth with Ben, chiefly about items stated in the disclosure. The SEC wanted clarification or they pointed out where Ben had gone wrong with compliance or something else. Marty told Ben that a typical comment letter generally includes 20 or so questions. Ben's submission was, apparently, very confusing for the folk at the SEC and their comment letter was very long—multiples of the usual length.

Eventually, Ben was able to get a sign-off from the SEC allowing him to do a public offering. A good result, but not great. Ben found out, to his consternation, it was not a "covered security," meaning that he had to get it cleared by every state. He started filing in other states, which was a challenge; his application was novel, and the states are not staffed in the same way as the SEC. They are not often involved in public offerings. Indeed, what Ben was filing was not technically a public offering. Under Regulation A, they were filing for a private offering that was being made available to the public, as illogical as that may sound.

What had helped facilitate the process at the SEC was that the building Ben was buying and renovating was down the street from the SEC building. The staffers were able to walk down and see the development site, which made it both tangible and interesting. Something out of the ordinary that made their day-to-day routine a little more thought-provocative. Ben thinks, and hopes, that they enjoyed the process as much as he did. His wasn't the normal filing that might be a $10 billion company or more. He was raising $325,000 and it felt to Ben like he was nothing more than the lonely guy alongside the megacompanies usually encamped at the SEC.

The first offering cleared the process in August 2012, less than four months after the passing of the JOBS Act. Ben's idea to sell to the general public was already getting into the zeitgeist. He realized that he wasn't the only person thinking that the system was broken and that it needed an alternative and that people were wondering what the Internet could do. By late 2011 his idea, in different forms expressed by different people, had hit the House of Representatives. Ben remembers how quickly it got to the House, passed there, and went to the president to sign. He recalls that it moved at an exceptional speed.

Ben was invited to visit the Hill. Senators Brown and Warner were championing a capital formation bill, Ben remembers, and it was going to get passed by the Senate. Senator Markley wanted to water it down, which would have killed it. There was an ensuing struggle between the middle-of-the-road Democratic Party and the left Democratic Party senators. Ben gave testimony and talked about his experience and what he was doing.

His case was unusual in that he had a tangible example. It was there that Ben met a fellow from Wefunder who was also giving testimony, and there were two or three random people up on the Hill who were trying to make the bill happen. These included people, though Ben never really got to know any of them, who were to start a crowdfunding community once the Act passed. Ben was never in that community because what he was doing in real estate was something different.

Ben isn't sure how he ended up getting involved on the Hill. He had a website and was busy with the SEC—basically raising money from the crowd. Some of his investors were highly visible and he had all sorts of random people who had invested in his deal. Aneesh Chopra, Obama's CTO, invested in the deal. Maybe having launched the first-ever real estate crowdfunding deal must have spread the word and someone suggested that Ben should be part of the conversation.

Ben's time on the Hill was spent mostly on the Senate side. In the House it happened so fast and, when it hit the Senate, people like Ben thought it would die. To help avoid such a fate, Ben reached out to Senator Warner, who asked that he come up to the Senate to explain what he was doing.

Crowdfunding equity wasn't easy to explain. The idea was very ephemeral in the beginning. People didn't understand what it meant. Ben was the man to explain it. He went to Senator Brown's office, where he met with the senator's staffers. He met with Merkley's office and with Warner's people. One thing led to another. Staffers, once they heard his story, would walk him over to someone else. He told them what he was doing, why he was doing it, how it worked, and why it made sense. He knew it was just one unique application of the idea of selling securities to the general public. But his was a real, concrete application of the idea.

The whole thing was a new idea for everyone. He imagined that the challenge of explaining it was similar to trying to explain social media before it existed. No one understood social media before it happened. The idea that there was a regulation that would make something happen didn't necessarily help people imagine what it might look like. They wondered why somebody would invest or raise money this way, and what would be some of the benefits. They wanted to know what some of the issues were that needed to be fixed and that was one of the main reasons they were interested in talking to Ben—he had an existent example that was moving forward. He was not only dealing with the implementation of the idea with the general public but had also already dealt with the SEC and with the states.

The offering that Ben had submitted successfully to the SEC had taken a year and a half to do. He had raised $325,000 for the deal, gone through submissions with the SEC, applied to the states, and had spent $150,000 getting there. He realized that things shouldn't and couldn't be this difficult; he was keen to see the JOBS Act pass so that he could scale. It was encouraging to him that he had been able to meet directly with senators and their staff and had found them to be responsive. At one point, the questions became politicized around investor protections. Ben thought that people were fearmongering for a short period, but because the speed and momentum was so fast and the crisis in the country was so extreme, he found that people were willing to take risks around innovation. People wanted to fix things. People wanted to do something.

There were other people on the Hill that Ben came across who were supportive of the bills. Mike Norman, who co-founded Wefunder, was there, and Ben remembers coming across Woodie Neiss, who later formed an association for crowdfunders. Ben never really thought of himself as a crowdfunder, thinking what he was doing as nothing more than online syndication. Crowdfunding sounds to Ben like donation. Even so, he was aware of only two or three other people on the Hill advocating for it and he just happened to be the only one who was doing it at the time.

Ben was invited to the Rose Garden signing but couldn't go—his day job took precedence. The irony of its passing was that, for Ben, it didn't help in any material way for years. Once it passed, the SEC didn't write the rules, get comments on the rules, and then promulgate the rules for another two to three years. Ben was hardly surprised. Having been through an application with the SEC, he knew that the processes were really complicated. People don't always understand how complicated these things can be to craft and Ben knew that the SEC also had to finish Dodd Frank, among other legislation.

To go on with raising capital for additional real estate deals Ben, at first, continued down the same path using the same regulations and submissions he had done for the first deal. It wasn't any easier the second and third time around. The problem was that what they were doing was never meant to be done at scale. Ben had jerry-rigged some old regulations but knew that it wasn't a high-traffic solution.

The JOBS Act held out a lot of promise for Ben; it might resolve some of these problems, but initially there were a number of false-positive realizations of what could be done. At the beginning there was a lot of excitement but not a lot of actualization.

The Act was signed into law in April 2012. Ben had done one deal before, and then started using Regulation D to do a few more deals that remained small in 2013 and 2014. In 2015 the SEC finally promulgated the new Regulation A+ change—the old version of which was the regulation that Ben had been using pre-JOBS Act. Ben thinks that the SEC did a great job with Regulation A because they had fixed everything in it that had not worked previously. He had an offering fully prepared and ready for the moment Regulation A+ became available, and when it did, he filed immediately. Even then, there were all sorts of random things they had to deal with and many things they had to create—defining what a transaction might look like for buying an investment online, or how a checkout works, or what exactly is an investor signing, or what is the privacy policy?

Ben and his team had written answers to all these questions in their pre-JOBS Act filings during 2011 and 2012. Their writings had become templates for the definition of real estate crowdfunding. Filing under Regulation A+, they were given the opportunity to refine the responses. In effect, they co-wrote the regulations with the SEC. Ben was the guinea pig that tested the first Regulation A offerings and helped to hone the regulations that define it.

That's not to say that Ben and his team were working with the SEC in any formal way. In some ways they were nobodies; the SEC typically deals with massive transactions like those with oil giants like Exxon or Shell. Compared to them, Fundrise was nothing more than an ant on an elephant. But because this was so visible a set of regulations at the time, and because Fundrise was actually putting it into practice in a real way, it was helpful to the SEC to see it in action. The SEC could see all the problems Ben was facing and struggling earnestly to fix. This made rewriting the rules a lot easier because it wasn't theory, but practical. The SEC could see exactly what was wrong with it.

Once the filing was approved, Fundrise remained cautious about openly advertising because they weren't clear on the best course of action or the legal side. They had their own way, of course, to market the platform to increase awareness, but found even that was a process with the SEC. Ben remembers when his team first posted on Facebook. The initial response from the SEC came in a comment letter; they insisted that Fundrise had to have a link to the SEC public filing directly from the Facebook advertisement—or from Twitter or Instagram or any other platform. With any social media advertising there is only one link that is allowed, so to have that one link push directly to the SEC.gov website made no sense. Everything was novel, and Ben and his team had to work through it all.

After the first Regulation A+ filing, Fundrise started to build in scale over the course of three or four years. They had two thousand investors in the three years from 2012 to the end of 2015, but it wasn't until 2015 that they finally got their initial Regulation A+ approved. When they launched it, they had ten thousand new investors in the first 48 hours. This was, in short, a far better way to achieve Ben's vision than anything he had earlier conceived and had been doing before.

The fundamental change for Fundrise from Regulation A+ was that previously they had two options: either to solicit only high-net-worth individuals (the 1 percent) or, alternatively, go through 50 states and the SEC to be able to do a national Internet offering. That was also very difficult and cumbersome. In either of these cases Ben couldn't really scale because there were, on the one hand, too few people or, on the other hand, a very torturous process.

The new Regulation A+ allows Fundrise to do a national offering with just the SEC. Anybody can invest in it. The Regulation fully democratized real estate investing. For Ben and Fundrise, it has been the fulfillment of his vision to bring an alternate system to capital formation, lower the costs, increase reliability and trust, and make real estate investing accessible to everyone. For Ben it is the alternative to the system he feels failed him and so many others in 2008.

10

RealtyShares: Nav Athwal

Nav Athwal started his career as an engineer, so his early work experience was in technology rather than real estate. He worked as an electrical engineer for a company in Oakland right out of college and was living in the Bay Area, exploring that side of the world. He'd always had an interest in exploring the real estate market since his father was a broker and investor, so while he was still an engineer, he got his real estate broker's license and began selling single-family homes and small commercial buildings and helping folk get refinances at a time when the market was still good but the economy was about to enter the recession.

He sold real estate to make extra money and, because he really loved the tangible nature of real estate, became hooked on it. When the recession of 2008–2009 hit he thought it would be a good time to take a different approach to real estate, so he went to law school at University of California Berkeley. He knew going into it that he wanted to focus on working at a law firm for a few years where he could learn the intricacies of transactional real estate and entitlements. His hope was to one day be a real estate developer and an avid and active real estate investor.

He graduated from law school in 2010 at the time when the economy was just getting out of the recession and things were beginning to improve. He started working for a law firm in San Francisco called Farella, Braun and Martel. The firm had about two hundred attorneys, and Nav was in the land use real estate group, where he concentrated on entitlement work and in assisting developers with getting their entitlements and permits to build multifamily commercial projects in and around San Francisco. He was also working with solar companies, helping them aggregate property rights so they could build utility-scale solar projects. At the same time, he was also doing various transactional real estate work such as easements, leases, and purchase and sale agreements. It was a good time to be in real estate; San Francisco was booming again. There were a lot of new projects in the pipeline that had stalled during the recession, and Nav's clients were very sophisticated public and private institutions like Real Estate Investment Trusts (REITs) and other large funds. It was a great place for Nav to learn a lot about the real estate market.

At the same time, he knew he wanted to do something more entrepreneurial; his goal had always been to do something in the development world. But he knew development was complex, so he thought the best way to start would be to invest in existing assets while still working at his law firm. He started looking to buy value-added apartment buildings and single-family homes with existing cash flow. At that time in 2010–2012 there were a lot of opportunities to buy properties at great prices.

He was able to assemble a portfolio of seven or eight properties, but often when he saw an amazing deal, raising capital was a bottleneck. The process of creating presentation materials and going to multiple individual investors and trying to convince them that he had found a good deal was time-consuming and unproductive. Because of this, Nav couldn't move fast enough on the capital side to execute on these deals and consequently lost a lot of them just because he didn't have the capital or the time to raise it efficiently.

He was talking to one of his buddies from Berkeley who had been at business school while Nav was at a law school and with whom he had tried to put together a single-family Real Estate Owned (REO) fund. Nav mentioned his challenges with raising capital to the friend and suggested that they begin to think about innovative ways to do this. Why not leverage technology to build a platform where they could raise the capital through a broad distribution of investors with whom they didn't have prior access? He'd already noticed that investors in a good real estate deal are usually located within a small radius of where the sponsor lives or works and where the deal is located. Typically, it was difficult to go beyond that. He found real estate investing to be hyperlocal and he wanted to change that and give investors more opportunities to diversify and developers access to a broader base of investors.

Nav and his buddy from Berkeley got excited about the idea of using a technology platform because it gave them a way to raise capital. After doing some research, they knew there were a lot of investors putting their money into mutual funds and stocks because they did not have access to alternative investments. Real estate is not only the largest asset class in the world, but also the largest alternative investment sought after by individual investors. It became a perfect storm: having investors who wanted access to deals and operators who wanted access to capital. Nav and his friend realized that they could create a connection point between these two constituencies by using technology.

Initially, the goal was to just do this for their own deals, but they quickly started thinking a lot bigger; this idea could be broadly applied to investors and operators around the country. When the idea was formulated back in 2012 they had no wind of the JOBS Act and no clue that it even existed. They were focused on how their idea would work, not only from the technology side but also from the legal side—which is where a lot of the complexity is. Once they started digging in they realized doing what they were contemplating would be considered a sale of securities, which fell under the Securities Act of 1933. They would have to either register the securities or operate under an exemption. That's when they first heard about the JOBS Act, which passed in April 2012, a few months after they had conceived their idea.

Nav had started researching how the securities laws worked and how they were impacted by online platform technology. He read articles and had come across some legislative notes on the JOBS Act. Once he and his friend found out about that they joined an e-mail group of other people who were thinking about similar ideas, though not in real estate, and started having conversations to learn as much as they could.

Their goal at the time was to create a platform, ultimately to be called RealtyShares, that could be accessed by any investor anywhere, enabling them to be able to invest any amount they wanted into a private real estate deal located hundreds or even thousands of miles away. Nav was excited about

Title III of the Act, which would allow for the sale of securities to individual, retail, non-accredited investors, which had until then been prohibited except for registered offerings. There were other benefits of the Act, such as those contained in Title II, which was to permit general solicitation of securities under the private placement exemption. And then there was Title IV, which allowed for raising large funds up to $50 million.

The Act was exciting to Nav, but he was cautious at the same time having studied administrative law as a law student and knowing that it can take a long time between when a law goes into effect until it actually becomes operable. He was not holding his breath for this to happen and told his co-founder that it was going to be critical that they find a way to operate under pre-JOBS Act laws, otherwise it may be three years or more before they would be able to execute on their platform. They did some research into agency no-action letters that had been given to Funders Club and Angels List on how to do what they wanted to do under the existing Rule 506(b) private placement exemption.

Their lawyers and their research told them that they could do what they wanted, and while they would not be allowed to advertise their deals, they could promote them behind a login where they had to first verify that an investor signing up was accredited and met the standards of an accredited investor that the SEC had promulgated. Although this would not allow them to experience the full vision they had originally intended, which was to build a mass market platform, it did allow them to at least get a start, to prove out the market, and to raise some money. Their ultimate vision came into sight at the beginning of 2013 when they started working on the technology build-out, bringing in their first engineer and, fast forward six months, when they launched their first set of deals using 506(b).

Their first two deals were tiny, single-family debt deals. They chose to start there because, although most of the platforms today have become commercial in their focus, financing apartment buildings, retail centers, hotels, and so on, when Nav first started with individual investors, capital was the biggest constraint and he needed to be able to convince these folk that they should invest in the deal. The best way to do this, he reasoned, was to show investors liquidity quickly so that they could see that the model works full cycle.

To achieve this objective Nav and his co-founder chose short-duration, single-family fix-and-flip loans because it was a great time in the real estate cycle, around 2013, for those kinds of loans. Banks were not in that market and hard-money lenders were not back in the market yet, so it was a perfect opportunity for Nav to fill a gap in the market and to generate some attractive yields with interest rates in the 9–12 percent range for prime borrowers. Plus, these loans were 6–12 months in duration, so the short term provided quick exits for investors. Another reason they started with loans like these was because they needed capital of anywhere from $100,000 to $500,000, so not a lot of capital per deal, and investors would start seeing returns immediately, which would show them that the model works.

Nav understood the most important driver for his platform would be how to win the trust of his investors, and then maintain it once won. He asked himself how he could keep investors coming back and wanting to invest more, because that's what would lead to the success or ultimate potential failure of his platform. Working with these smaller, high-yield loans with quick exits helped him get up and running.

Toward the end of 2012 after Nav and his co-founder had conceived of the idea and started working on it, they were both still at their day jobs, so the going was a little slower than others. Fundrise was the first platform Nav learned of. There was an article that came out in a journal about this new platform that had just funded a deal. Fundrise was financing in Washington DC using crowdfunded capital. Reading the article got Nav both nervous and excited at the same time: nervous because he is a very competitive person and felt they were behind when they wanted to be the first to market, but excited because he knew there was going to be a level of interest from folk given this article and Fundrise's success. The article validated the model for him.

Right around this time and when Nav was launching his own first deal he got wind of another platform, RealtyMogul, which was probably the second in the space and initiating a very similar concept. Those two platforms were the only ones Nav was aware of before he went to market, which was around two months after RealtyMogul. By the end of 2012 and going into 2013 they started to see more real-estate-specific platforms emerge. It was an exciting time, but also one that made Nav realize he needed to put up or shut up, and that he needed to get into this full time and really make it work or just let others who were already ahead of him do what they were doing.

Nav was still an attorney at the time, moonlighting, but after he and his co-founder funded the first few deals, he believed the idea could work even though it would take time to ramp up. He was confident that the idea had a lot of legs and that it would be really interesting. His co-founder, however, decided he wasn't going to go full time. He couldn't leave his day job because he had financial obligations that didn't allow him to do so.

So in August of 2013 they parted ways and Nav went full time, bringing in a full-time engineer and another gentleman to help run business development and some of the operational needs. At this time they entered 500 Startups, which is an incubator based out of Mountain View in Silicon Valley. They went into the incubator still very unsure if the idea would work. They had funded a few small deals and overcome the legal issues, figuring out how to make it work, but what kept them up at night was how to scale and ramp up, how to take a platform that was connecting investors with real estate deals and with operators they had never met and convince them to invest. Nav needed to know how to scale the business to a point where it would actually make a dent in the real estate market: a market that measured in the trillions of dollars, yet where he and his co-founder were barely operating in the thousands.

They decided to broaden their focus, and in a test case at the end of 2013, launched their first multifamily deal. Whereas their single-family debt deals funded within a few days to maybe a few weeks, their trial multifamily deal sat on the platform for at least two months, barely getting funded. They learned their investors wanted a short-term, relatively liquid investment and were not ready yet to put money into a deal that may be five or seven years before maturity, even if it seemed very attractive and was located in a very strong market. It was a good learning experience for Nav and his team. They refocused on the single-family debt market for a little while longer until they had garnered more trust and had built up a bigger base of capital. At the time, they were not spending much on marketing. Most of their deals and investors were coming through word of mouth, referrals, and PR. They received a tremendous amount of PR going into 2014 and that really helped them build their initial base of customers. It was helpful, because it was very cost-effective for them.

By the second quarter of 2014 they had raised about $2 million in venture capital from General Catalyst, who lead the round along with friends and family and angels. Nav was feeling good that he had the capital that would allow him to continue to prove out his model. At that point he had raised maybe another $10 million on the platform for investment in real estate deals, which is nothing significant in terms of real estate capital markets, but it was enough to prove that the idea could work and it built a foundation of trust within their investor and developer base he and his team could continue strengthening.

At that point they decided it was probably the right time to start introducing more commercial assets, so they hired a commercial underwriting investments team. The second time around it still wasn't easy, but they started to see a lot more success. The initial commercial deal they launched was on a large multifamily complex in Texas, near the Dallas Cowboys' practice stadium. It was a very nice class-A asset, but large, so they were only able to take a minority position in the deal, and difficult for an individual investor to understand. Going forward, they chose instead to start doing smaller deals where their investor capital would be the majority a sponsor required for any given deal. This would give Nav greater leverage over the terms of the deal, making it more compelling for investors and easier to explain.

This resonated with their investor base, so that's where they started to focus. They did a broad swath of deals in multifamily, retail, and industrial in California, Texas, New York, and Florida. Most of their deals ended up being multifamily, which is still the trend today on RealtyShares, with some 70 percent of the deals being multifamily. They tend to work because, one, there's less risk with that product type than retail or office and, two, there is a stable cash flow from day 1. Plus, multifamily is one of the largest asset classes within the commercial real estate space. Nav and his team started focusing on this type of asset while still doing the single-family debt, and then started to hit an inflection point. In their first year, 2014, they raised funds totaling $22 million; the next year it was $80 million, and the following year $200 million.

Another factor in building their platform was structuring their deals where each equity deal had its own LLC. For an investor in an apartment building, the way it works on the RealtyShares site is that they become a member of an LLC managed by RealtyShares, and that LLC acts as a single investor that would then invest in the second LLC that actually owns the property. RealtyShares investors are not direct owners of the LLC and holding the title of the property; rather, they are one step removed. Nav and his team initiated this structure because if a developer took a bunch of $5000 and $10,000 level investors directly into the LLC, it would create a pretty big administrative headache and not be in alignment with how Nav pitched the deals. His proposition to developers was that capital raising had been inefficient, difficult, and time-consuming in the past. "Let us turn that process into an afterthought," he'd tell developers, "you come to us, we will qualify you, and we will bring one check to you in a matter of weeks rather than the months it would take if you're doing it offline."

This was a compelling scenario for developers, since it delivered value, while the idea of managing many small investors did not. The structure Nav created was designed to alleviate that problem. The debt side was a little different. Nav and his team had what is called a limited recourse note offering something similar to what Lending Club and Prosper had used that allowed them to be a little bit more efficient. They didn't have to create a new LLC for every deal they did.

This was what they focused on for the first year and a half and then going into 2015 they raised another $10 million of capital under a Series A from Menlo Ventures. They were successful in raising this round because they had proven there was a market for individual retail accredited investors and wanted to move to their next growth phase. They had sponsors and developers convinced this was a really efficient way to raise capital. But there were two things they really needed to do. One, they needed to bring more capital to a deal because once they moved into commercial real estate, bringing $1 million wasn't meaningful enough. They needed to focus on check sizes in the $1–5 million range. Two, they probably needed to bring additional sources of capital beyond self-directed accredited investors because it wasn't going to be enough to help them scale and grow the business. Those two realizations became challenges they wanted to solve over the next year and a half after they had raised the Series A. They knew that the institutional market was there because they had seen it with Lending Club and Prosper. And they noticed that a majority of the capital on those platforms came from institutions.

The reason they thought what they were selling would be of interest to institutions was because their focus from day 1, and their thesis from day 1, was as follows. In the institutional sphere deals are often done in core markets like San Francisco, New York, and Los Angeles, and they're of a certain size: maybe they are $50 million, maybe they are $100 million. Institutions want to be in those larger assets because they can write large checks while doing the same amount of work as they would have to do if they had invested a much smaller amount. Institutions are far less present below the threshold of $50 or so million, which is where 85 percent of the annual transaction volume in the United States is, making it the largest part of the market from a unit perspective and half of the market from a dollar perspective.

Nav wanted to focus in the below $50 million range and build a very efficient, robust source of capital for that subinstitutional market. He noticed that the reasons institutions didn't participate at this level was that, one, developers might be perceived as less sophisticated or that the institutions were just not able to get to know the developers as much, and, two, institutions just don't want to do due diligence on a deal where they're only going to be putting in a $5–10 million check. RealtyShares' pitch to the institutions was that if they invested through the platform, RealtyShares would provide the underwriting and sourcing infrastructure for them so they could invest $50 million across ten deals rather than into just one, get more diversification, and do that just as efficiently as if they were putting this amount into just a single deal.

Initially the idea started to resonate with institutions more so on the debt side than on the equity, although once equity started getting more attention, it accelerated RealtyShares' ability to start generating more deals and put larger checks to work. RealtyShares did some deals with institutions and the "crowd," accredited individual investors, participating together. They also did some deals where the deal was crowd only or institutions only. Which deals went into which buckets was based mainly on the types of deals best suited to each type of investor, the crowd or the institutional capital. To be fair and avoid conflict with how they allocated capital, RealtyShares' credit team did a round robin for some of the platform's deals to ensure each type of capital was getting equal access to similar deals.

At the same time they were very focused on growing their accredited investor base and brought on a robust digital marketing team that was doing everything from Search Engine Marketing (SEM) to Facebook to referral to affiliate marketing, just to build up their accredited investor database. With this focus, RealtyShares' was able to build a base of 7000 active accredited investors. These investors participated in the marketplace, investing as little as $1000 and up to $100,000 plus at a time, building their portfolios and doing it 100 percent digitally—which included everything from signing up to verifying their accreditation, from going through a little FAQ and an anti-money laundering check to viewing deals to downloading and viewing documents and pictures. The whole thing as a completely digital process.

RealtyShares had a lot of really good feedback early on from investors telling them this was the easiest platform they had ever used to invest in anything, let alone real estate. They were told real estate investing this way was as easy as investing in stocks, which was exciting. The great stories out in the press at that time really helped. CNBC did some coverage when RealtyShares helped a man who had left his job as an engineer and wanted to get into fix and flipping. He had an amazing credit score but couldn't get money from banks. RealtyShares helped him do his first seven deals and he was very successful, paying them every time, on time. Yahoo News did a story on them when they helped a Facebook engineer who was completely terrified of the stock market and was looking to diversify but didn't know where to go. She wanted to invest in real estate but didn't have time to buy an asset outright and operate it. RealtyShares helped her put $100,000 plus to work across a variety of deals so she could earn passive income. Press coverage showing RealtyShares helping to change the lives of borrowers and developers and investors who didn't know how to diversify their portfolios or allocate capital to their deals before the platform really helped move the needle for RealtyShares. From the seat Nav was sitting in, this was very rewarding.

The other interesting piece for his platform was that once someone invested and built a portfolio, Nav wanted the experience to be very similar to how that investor would view their stock portfolio if they were logged into E-Trade. To accomplish this, RealtyShares built return charts, financial metrics, and data into the investor dashboard. An investor could see what deals they had put their money into, see how those deals were performing, get updates, and review their tax and legal documents, all from the convenience of their tablet or laptop. They could download a monthly account summary and earnings statement and see how returns were differing month to month using some visual charts. The experience was akin to what an investor would see on a stock trading platform, and this resonated with investors.

As the platform grew in this way, Nav raised two additional rounds of capital. At the end of 2015 he raised about $20 million of Series B capital from Union Square Ventures, who are big marketplace investors that really liked what RealtyShares was doing. Then they raised another $27 million in Series C capital in 2017. All in all, they were well capitalized and the team grew to about 75 people, almost all in San Francisco, except for a few folk in New York or who work at remote locations.

Nav is proud that the company has a great culture and a great group of people, and their DNA is a mix of technology and real estate folk. Building a platform of the type Nav built requires a lot of knowledge about how the real estate capital markets work, and how to underwrite, so it is really critical for his team to build that into their DNA, but also to not forget that they are innovating within the space and not just recreating a slightly better mousetrap. So he built a team from the outset to be a mix of people who are strong both in real estate and in technology.

Nav thinks the industry will continue to see a lot of innovation, not just from RealtyShares, but from others like RealtyShares, whether their model is either similar or very different. For example, he notices that Fundrise and RealtyMogul have taken the approach of building large funds or REITs and allowing non-accredited investors to participate and put capital to work across a broad spectrum of deals. He thinks there are a lot of very interesting things happening, and that it's going to change the real estate industry in a lot of ways. One way he sees change coming is that a lot more transparency and efficiency will be created in the industry, particularly around fees being charged by developers, for example.

RealtyShares and platforms like it are going to change how real estate capital markets work because such platforms are becoming something larger operators are recognizing as a way to potentially raise capital. They are creating an entirely new ecosystem within private real estate. Before, if an investor wanted to get real estate exposure, a public REIT was the only real way to do it passively. Crowdfunding is a new way. It is a new model to get direct ownership of real estate in a much more transparent way, where the investors can control the process from end to end. Nav thinks it's also going to stimulate further changes in the laws and regulations. When someone like Nav is building technology faster than the regulators can adapt to, they pay attention and quickly try to catch up. Nav believes this trend is what led to the JOBS Act and will lead to additional legislation down the line that takes into account how the real estate market is evolving to the way that business works; it is no longer just pen and paper. Real estate has become digital, and laws and regulations need to fit within that digital landscape.

The JOBS Act had a strong impact on the success of RealtyShares, but not in the way one might expect. Even today the platform operates under pre-JOBS Act exemptions. The company has done the occasional 506(c) deal, which emanated from the Act, but it was wasn't until Title II went into effect in late summer of 2014 that the JOBS Act delivered the first meaningful regulations to platforms of Nav's type that actually meant there was a new way to do business. Some platforms took advantage of Title II allowing them to advertise their offerings and publicly solicit instead of having everything behind a firewall. But using Title II to solicit the general public was not something that RealtyShares did right away because doing so brought with it additional burdens and obligations, like verifying accreditation. Whereas 506(b), the pre-JOBS Act predecessor regulation, allowed for self-verification of accreditations in a kind of check-box format, accreditations under 506(c) required platforms to take additional steps like examining accounting statements and balance sheets and tax documents. Nav thought these steps were too intrusive at a time when the industry was still very young.

He saw RealtyMogul use the new regulation in what he thought was a gimmicky deal, but one that worked well. It was a Hard Rock deal they did in California, where they used 506(c) for the offering. It garnered a lot more press and became highly visible. RealtyShares decided not to use this new regulation, except for maybe three or four deals just to test the model. The goal was to broaden their platform, and the reason they chose not to use the regulation was because they didn't want to create more hurdles in the path of investors who were potentially already uncomfortable investing online in a deal with an operator they had never met.

Industry growth was and continues to be evolutionary, says Nav. Fundrise has gone into Title IV territory using Regulation A+. They were the first ones to go there with non-accredited investors, followed by RealtyMogul. RealtyShares almost went there and then pulled back because what they learned, and Nav believes the industry needs to be cognizant of, is that individual investors are fantastic, but there is also a high cost involved with supporting that base of capital because there are so many investors and, at any time, there are going to be a lot of questions and comments the platform must handle.

Even though he did not directly use JOBS Act regulations, Nav sees that the Act has definitely broadened what his company was capable of doing online. In theory, his platform could exist and operate and build a big business without the JOBS Act, but with the JOBS Act, he and his team were able to build and scale an even bigger business much more quickly. The passing of the Act created momentum. It created an ecosystem, because even before the

Act was passed, the promise of the Act was there; the hope was there. That's what helped elevate platforms like RealtyShares to be confident enough to believe they had a viable model to pursue, that they could make it work because there was legislation with bipartisan support that would promote the building of online investment platforms.

RealtyShares would still exist without the JOBS Act, Nav thinks, but the company would not have been as successful if they had not had momentum from the passing of the Act. And the new industry of real estate crowdfunding itself would not be as large as it is if it had not been for the JOBS Act being passing into law, even if RealtyShares and other platforms could exist without it.

* * *

On November 7, 2018, RealtyShares announced that it had been unable to "secure additional capital" to continue funding its growth. By that time, the company had raised an excess of $60 million from some of the most influential venture capital funds in the world and financed close to $1 billion of real estate transactions.

As discussed in the conclusions section of this book, it is inevitable that companies in this nascent industry will fail. Business models are being tested for viability. We can assume other platforms will also flounder but for different reasons when their approach is found to be unsustainable.

Some will fail because the deals they list are poorly conceived, poorly underwritten, or poorly promoted by either themselves or the project sponsor. Their financial structure may become tenuous when exposed to vulnerability as the real estate market cycles downward. Some will simply be unable to sustain sufficient investor or developer acquisition velocity.

RealtyShares failed because they sought out and allowed the capital upon which their business model was reliant to dictate how the business was built. Rather than taking a lesson from their own playbook by providing immediate returns to investors and seeking to generate positive cash flow early in their lifecycle, they were instead subjected to the high-octane world of tech startups seeking super-rapid growth at the expense of making early-stage profit, and consequently veered away from the sedate real estate world where a steady, long-term perspective with steady cash-flow management is the key to longevity and wealth.

The closure of RealtyShares is not an indictment of the entire real estate crowdfunding industry, but rather a symbol of the natural growing pains of a brand new industry. Undoubtedly, others will heed the lessons learned from RealtyShares' failure, adapt their models accordingly, and attempt to avoid a similar fate.

As in all revolutions, evolution will take hold and only the fittest will survive to become the ultimate leaders of the crowd.

11

Investor: Ian Ippolito

Ian's first taste of real estate investing was with rental properties in the late 1990s, and with it came the realization that it could make him money. He took an online real estate course to learn how to run rental properties and continued investing, but became distracted as he was an entrepreneur and was able to make lot higher returns building companies and startups.

In 2006 he got into his first real estate syndication; at that time, it was not on the Internet. It was an old school syndication that turned out to be a bad investment that he later came to regret. He didn't know what he was doing, but learned a lot of good lessons about market cycles. It took him almost ten years to get out of that deal, barely breaking even when he did. He remained focused on his primary business, Vworker, which he sold in 2013 to an Australian company. He had a nice payout and was technically retired, though his new job was figuring out how to manage investments for himself and his family because that was now his sole income.

The stock market was still pretty volatile at the time and the Great Recession was not too far back in the rearview mirror, but things were changing and a host of alternative investments were coming out that piqued Ian's interest. He thought maybe there was more to the investment puzzle than the traditional advice to place X percent of his money in stocks and Y percent in bonds and not worry about other opportunities. He knew many people who'd had serious investment problems during the Great Recession and lost a lot of money. Indeed, he knew people who had to downsize their lifestyles or even lost their home, so he understood there was danger in volatility and he wanted to find ways to manage that volatility.

First, he started experimenting in Lending Club. This alternative investment platform pooled people's money together to make personal loans to individuals since, at that time, the banks had largely stopped doing so. The idea was that Lending Club was going to remove the bank as a middleman and provide investors the ability to be the bank, thereby, theoretically, earning higher returns than putting their money in a Certificate of Deposit (CD) with a low yield.

But Ian also wanted to diversify, which seemed possible through the newly discovered avenue of real estate crowdfunding. He was struck by the idea because, in some ways, it was very similar to Lending Club. Lending Club was, however, a lot more mature. With real estate crowdfunding there were a lot of inconveniences or other difficulties that made it seem a lot less safe at the time. The industry was simply too nascent.

To figure out this new investment channel Ian started running Google searches and looking up reviews on real estate crowdfunding sites. Not being able to find any, he realized he was going to have to do some more digging. Someone in a chat room he frequented mentioned a few sites, so he started looking at those companies and became increasingly interested in the opportunity. The sites made investing in real estate sound less volatile, which appealed to Ian, but he was concerned that he had no idea if what they were telling him was true or not since they were brand new companies without data he could check. He wondered if they were legally able to offer these deals, since what they were doing had previously been prohibited. Ian realized he would need to do a lot more research before feeling comfortable enough to put money in this investment channel.

His opinions were colored not only because of the recent recession, but also because of his bad prior experience with real estate syndication. Even so, there was something different about what he was seeing with real estate crowdfunding and he wanted to know more. He started approaching the opportunity much more cautiously than he had done with Lending Club, where he had just jumped in and invested right away. With real estate crowdfunding he was unwilling to put down even a single dollar until he had really checked it out.

When he started he really knew and understood very little, so the first thing he did was look at all the legal agreements, which were, of course, huge. He didn't know much about what he was looking at, so he took them to an attorney for review even though he didn't even know how to pick the right attorney. He didn't get the greatest advice and, looking back, he realizes that the firm he selected wasn't an expert in the field of real estate syndications. His attorneys gave him advice similar to what Ian got on his 2006 syndication: that if he really liked and trusted the sponsor, he might go ahead and make the investment, even though there could be a lot of leeway for the sponsor to go outside the boundaries of the investment pitch deck. The attorneys concluded by saying, from a legal point they couldn't really help much one way or the other.

Ian was also concerned about the legitimacy of the various websites he was looking at, so he started looking into that, too. He remembers asking questions of the platforms directly and because they were so new, they would sometimes make their legal counsel available. After talking to a few he started to learn the jargon, discovering the difference between 506(b) versus 506(c), among other things. He learned that these two regulations speak to different ways of soliciting investors that consequently came with different marketing strategies and different requirements for things that he would have to do as an investor and that they had to do as platforms. He started expanding his research and as he became more familiar with the space eventually he was able to connect to some independent attorneys who he also asked for advice.

They explained to him the JOBS Act was the core reason the platforms could do what they were doing, which helped reassure Ian, but he didn't dive much deeper into the Act than that. He could see how convoluted the process was, how slowly it was being implemented, and that a lot of people in the industry were expressing disappointment. People had expected the JOBS Act to revolutionize everything and start creating jobs as the economy pulled out from the depths of the Great Recession. But a year had gone by while the SEC promulgated the rules, which was discouraging for platform founders. As an entrepreneur, Ian saw it from their perspective, empathizing that these start-ups in the crowdfunding space had to tell their investors they hadn't been able to do what they said they were going to do because they were still waiting for the regulations to be clarified. It took years to get anything reasonable that the sites could work with, and after that it took even longer to be able to include non-accredited investors.

Ian continued conducting research and was keen to find his first investment. He focused on researching the platforms to improve his understanding of the industry. Before putting his money into any deal, he decided to find every single site in the industry and compare them against each other. His caution was colored by some previous things he had been involved with. At first, he didn't really know what standards he would compare the sites against, but over time, he realized there were some really important things worthy of close examination.

Some sites seemed like they might go out of business at any time due to lack of transactional volume. What would happen to his money if that happened? Knowledgeable attorneys he spoke with said it might be unclear. His investment could get rolled up in some sort of bankruptcy, with creditors trying to get his money, since the fund was no longer managing it.

He noticed that some of the sites were very different as far as the amount of money they had received from venture capital firms and what they were willing to spend. For example, there were some sites that pre-funded their deals. They may have received some sort of external investment at the corporate level, would use that capital to pre-fund deals, and only then would offer the opportunity to invest out to the crowd. At first, Ian liked this structure. Such sites claimed that the advantage to an investor was that the platform would be motivated to vet deals sufficiently because if it was unable to raise sufficient capital from the crowd, it would be stuck in the deal. Other sites simply didn't have the financial capability to do this, or perhaps chose not to.

Looking back, Ian reflects that this might have been true, but it wasn't a 100 percent reliable safety net. One of the early pre-funding sites was ranked #1 for a few years because investors overwhelmingly raved about how well it had done for them. But then the site ran into financial trouble. When it did, perhaps the underwriting suffered, because investors started reporting lots of troubled deals. Ian ended up downgrading them despite their pre-funding. Pre-funding was a nice plus, but he saw how it wasn't a 100 percent guarantee.

These sites were pitching their integrity to him on the basis that they were putting their own money on the line, explaining to him that if he didn't invest, or if other people in the crowd didn't, that they would be the main investor in the deal. Ian was told that by several of the platforms who contrasted their approach with other sites that didn't pre-fund. "Look," he was told, "these other sites don't have confidence in their own deals." It was very compelling to Ian, especially in the early days. But over time, crowdfunding became so popular that deals were guaranteed to fill up. On one pre-funding site some deals would oversubscribe in under an hour. In those circumstances, the pre-funding wasn't much of a protection.

His overview of the industry took months to complete. He went into everything and interviewed people on every platform. Again, he was very gun shy. He talked to individual investors about their successful crowdfunding deals, their bad deals, and their favorite and least-favorite platforms. He networked. He found Internet sites where investors connected with each other trying to do deals. Some of them had invested in crowdfunding, so he connected with people individually on those sites. He did as much networking as he could and identified patterns that indicated some sites were better and some were worse. Some sites were very open and transparent, whereas others would not talk about anything and would not reveal any information. Although later sites did reveal how they were performing, none would at this time and this kept Ian from being comfortable with the idea of investing before he had more information.

He started giving copies of the results of his due diligence on all these platforms to other investors, who, in turn, started telling other people that there was a guy who had created rankings which had taken months to figure out. He received e-mails requesting a copy and, at some point, he decided to abandon individually e-mailing people and decided instead to create a website and put it up publicly (more below). His first investment wasn't a big play. Ian went in for the minimum because he was still hesitant and felt he didn't fully understand everything that was going on. But he was willing to dip in the water and make his first investment.

Later, upon reflection, he decided the investment wasn't premised on the right assumptions, so he decided to take a different approach. He didn't want to invest in something he didn't fully understand at the property level. Instead, he wanted to find something that was similar to his previous experiences in the 1990s with rental property investment. He couldn't underwrite a hotel deal, for example, and so he started looking at multifamily residential investing, which was something he did understand and could wrap his brain around. He wasn't alone in looking to invest in real estate online. Quite a few people were really excited about it. It was a brand new thing and the returns were great compared to other alternatives.

As his research progressed, he expanded his website. Originally, it was just the reviews he had written along with the site rankings, but then he realized he needed to put more information up so he didn't have to answer all the questions about the rankings. He added in-depth reviews of 30–40 sites and put up a spreadsheet that compared them against approximately 20 different data points as well as going pretty deeply into their individual DNA.

The biggest problem was that the minimum investments were high. It was the first thing he noticed, especially coming from Lending Club, where he could put in maybe a minimum of $20 per note. On Lending Club, an investor could take maybe $5000 or $6000 and have a hundred or more notes and be diversified. But on the real estate crowdfunding platform, that $5000 or $6000 might not get him into even one investment. Some sites had $10,000 and $25,000 minimums, which was a big problem for Ian. He actually complained about it to numerous sites and they never really gave him a good answer as to why they had such high minimums.

It wasn't until a couple of years later that he understood why. The high minimums weren't so much a limitation of crowdfunding, per se, nor were the minimums a limitation of the sites or the sponsors. Rather, there was a limitation on how many investors can typically buy into an LLC before the reporting requirements increased. The sites didn't really do a good job of explaining this to Ian.

Then there was the problem of low volume on most of the sites, with only one site doing commercial real estate that had a decent number of active deals. Back when Ian first started, good, industry-leading volume meant having maybe eight investments open at once. One site specializing in fix-and-flip hard-money loans had maybe 10 or 11 investments open at the same time. These were high-traffic sites back then, but the number of deals on a site quickly fell off to only one investment, and some had none. It was difficult with some sites to even tell when they had last had an investment listed. Their record might show that they had closed a whole bunch of deals, but there was nothing open. Ian thought a lot of people were perhaps trying to grow their platforms by exaggerating their experience to get investors interested.

Early on, every site he looked at was focused exclusively on individual deals; no one had funds at the time. Typically, most sites had small deals. Like a fix-and-flip deal of more than a hundred thousand dollars was a pretty big deal, and on the commercial side, they might be investing in something larger, but more than $1 million would have been considered a very large amount back then.

Deal structure also varied. There were debt sites, like the fix-and-flip sites, and there were equity sites. There were all sorts of varieties of equity on offer, so Ian had to learn the different types of preferred equity, among other things. Fees also varied dramatically. Some sites charged the sponsors, whereas others charged investors. Others set up new LLCs that were the sole investor in deals and that acted as conduits through which individual investors could interact with developers. There were other sites that connected the investor directly to the sponsor, and others still that were themselves the sponsors who were doing their own underwriting—they were both the sponsor and a platform at the same time. There was a lot of variety.

Ian learned a lot from his research, though his learning continues to evolve and he's not sure if some of his earlier requirements were as important as he thought they were at the time. He saw there were a handful of companies that seemed to have quite a bit of cash, and they seemed to be doing things the right way. Some sites were going the slow growth route and others were trying to grow quickly, and some platforms were starting slow but clearly spending a lot of money very quickly in anticipation of fast growth. At that time Ian thought that the sites having a big amount of venture funding behind them were less likely to disappear overnight, which is probably true to some extent. Since then, however, he has come to think how little he appreciated the amount of pressure that gets put on the companies to produce, especially if they have trouble raising additional rounds. Maybe that puts pressure on the caliber of their underwriting.

Another early mistake he made was in thinking the companies that interjected themselves between the investor and the sponsor were going to be the long-term winners because they were adding value, and that the other sites not doing this were little more than something off Craigslist with no added value. At first, some of these had the highest levels of investor satisfaction. Over time, however, he softened that view because investors started reporting problems that arose when a company was trying to stick themselves between the sponsor and investors. He saw that investors wanted information and were not getting it at all, or getting the wrong information, or not getting information on a timely basis. They were becoming very frustrated. Many of Ian's ideas have changed over time.

Again, Ian's perspective was that of an entrepreneur's. He understood from a business model perspective, it is generally preferable to have some sort of value. The problem with the Craigslist model, he believed, was that it had no sustainable value and the platform would end up being disintermediated. Ian knew this could be a concern for some startups; if they were disintermediated, they'd be out of business. It also made sense to protect their own business model by shielding investors from making direct contact with sponsors because if the platform owns the investors, the sponsor doesn't even know who the investors are and cannot approach them directly. If the platform holds themselves in that position, it gives them more power.

These considerations were all very important for Ian because he wanted to be sure the sites he invested on had a sustainable business model and were fundamentally stable so he didn't have to worry about them entering bankruptcy. After lengthy discussions with his attorneys, he came to realize that no matter what measures are taken to protect investors from worst-case scenarios, in the end, there is no way of knowing how robust the protections are until you actually go through a bankruptcy. Ian decided to protect himself as much as possible by avoiding questionable structures that might lend themselves to complications in bankruptcy or other worst-case situations.

These deep concerns drove Ian to ask platforms how they were doing and he was surprised to find most of them didn't want to talk about it. Many would not release any information. They wouldn't say how many deals they had done, talk about revenue, or indicate how many employees they had. Early on, the only thing he could get to determine a company's health was at the corporate level, and that was only with companies who had venture backing because they usually had some sort of press release about how much money they had raised.

In the early days, he also had more confidence in a platform if a venture fund had backed it because he assumed the fund had taken the time to do due diligence on the company and that they had spent a lot more hours on it than him. Having venture backing became one of his criteria for ranking. Later, he came to doubt the reliability of his assumption when many venture-backed companies were not able to raise additional rounds of capital and came under tremendous pressure to perform. As he started digging deeper into the newer deal underwriting he suspected some platforms have been compromised in order to build volume at the expense of quality.

In addition to pre-funding and venture backing, it was also important to Ian that a platform was transparent enough to at least answer his questions. There were some firms that were actually hostile to answering anything, so he quickly decided he was not going to deal with them. Despite wanting to invest more, doing so was difficult because the industry was so immature. The high minimums were an issue and he didn't want to put a large proportion of his net worth into something he felt was not diversified enough over geography, asset classes, and strategies. For example, there was nothing even close to what would be called a core-plus investment, let alone even a core investment. There were smaller properties on the equity investment side as well as on the debt side, but most properties were not in prime locations. Back then there were no opportunities for non-accredited investors either, so the pool of availability was really small. Ian complained to a lot of different platforms, giving them his two cents' worth. "Look at Lending Club," he said, "You guys can be so successful if you just copy them. They just completed a billion-dollar IPO. That could be you!"

In his own way he tried to incentivize them. He had access and was talking to the principals, but he knows now he didn't understand some of the limitations and pressures they were dealing with. A lot of recommendations never came about, but some of them did; others will take time.

12

RealtyMogul: Jilliene Helman

In the period before the JOBS Act was passed in 2012, Jilliene Helman worked for Union Bank and Bank of Tokyo-Mitsubishi, where she had spent most of her career on the wealth management side. She worked with private banking clients who had capital they wanted to invest, whether in stocks or bonds. In working on the wealth management side of the banking industry, she found that most of the wealthiest clients were real estate investors. They either made their money in real estate or had numerous real estate holdings. The bank obviously had a large lending arm, so these investors were very visible to Jilliene.

She grew up in a real estate family. Her grandfather built an apartment building in Los Angeles, her mother was in residential luxury real estate in Malibu, and her father owned real estate through his businesses. He was a serial entrepreneur. Not a real estate entrepreneur, but he owned commercial real estate, industrial real estate, and offices for his companies, so Jilliene had been exposed to real estate as a young person before she went to work in banking.

When the JOBS Act came out she was in the bank's Los Angeles office. When she read about it, the first thought she had was that there had to be a way to use this legislation in the real estate market. It was a very natural leap for her to realize it was the first time the securities laws had changed in 80 years, and that there was an opportunity to start selling real estate transactions on the Internet by utilizing some of the legislation in the JOBS Act.

Interestingly, she really didn't start using the JOBS Act or any of the new legislation until four years or so later, when RealtyMogul launched a Regulation A+ transaction. At the beginning, though, Jilliene realized there was going to be a lot of publicity and marketing around the changes. At the time, she was getting more and more involved in private real estate syndication. These were private deals where she could get a personal stake in a real estate transaction. What better way was there, than using this new piece of legislation, to reach a wider scope of the population and bring them private real estate transaction opportunities like the ones that had made so much wealth for her banking clients.

Jilliene knew that the JOBS Act was oriented to startups, but she also knew she wasn't going to raise money for startups. She knew nothing about the venture world at that point in time. Rather, she had an immediate eureka moment that the new regulations could be used to sell real estate on the Internet. She had grown up learning about passive income and hard assets, and she saw this was an opportunity to finance those hard assets, so it was immediately obvious to her that it would work for real estate. She saw in the Act a marketing opportunity.

The JOBS Act, for Jilliene when she started RealtyMogul, was just an opportunity to be able to market on the Internet, to solicit on the Internet, to identify investors using the Internet. In addition, the opportunity to conduct marketing around the very idea that there was a legislative change was itself newsworthy. She recalls it was similar to when Obamacare came out and new companies were created as a result. Regulations can stifle industries, but they can also force industries to innovate and change, and she saw that and was really excited about the possibilities.

After leaving banking in October 2012, she launched RealtyMogul; her first transaction closed in April 2013. She started off with a couple of transactions using the new Regulation 506(c), but soon realized it was really challenging to get investors comfortable with giving out all their financial information. The regulation had embedded in it a lot of hoops and a lot of hurdles, so they shifted to predominantly using 506(b), which was the original, unchanged regulation that was used pre-JOBS Act. In fact, Jilliene says she could have run her business prior to the JOBS Act coming out, because she chose to run what is called a "private network." She discovered that before the JOBS Act came out the SEC had issued the "Lamp no-action" letter that allowed platforms to get to know their customer and build a relationship online without ever meeting them in person.

The idea had been tried before with other companies pre-JOBS Act that had attempted to run these kinds of businesses, but they didn't have the media and the press wind in their sails. Jilliene realized when she saw the JOBS Act that it would cause tremendous interest in the press, and that once media started coming out and educating everybody on what crowdfunding was and creating legitimacy for the industry and legitimacy for brands like hers, it would be possible to actually accomplish these things.

She left the bank with a plan to build a digital marketplace for real estate investing. She started to build the company and sourced her first transaction while working with her Chief Technology Officer to build the first version of the website. When she started out, the process was very much one transaction, one investor, at a time. She remembers that she personally called and e-mailed the first two or three thousand investors to welcome them and, because she didn't have business phones, she was giving them her cell phone number. Jilliene and her co-founder built the company through one-on-one communication. Jilliene called a couple of thousand investors and her co-founder called a couple of thousand investors and they ran the business like a phone booth for the first year. Everyone in the whole company spent four or five hours a day calling on investors, and then they worked nights on the platform and on the technology while trying to build relationships.

Jilliene says "anytime you're starting a company, it's beg, kick and cry your way to trying to get people to do business with you." She needed a deal, and so she called a friend of hers, Nick Halaris, who owned a development company called AH Capital. She told him she was starting a company and needed some deals and asked if he could help her. The first deal RealtyMogul did was an AH Capital deal. It was a $110,000 transaction in Compton, which is really not a nice place in broader Los Angeles.

The first two years of the company was all favors. It was the first company she had ever started and she didn't know what to do, so she asked for favors. They really got off to the races when they started sourcing folk whom she had never known prior to starting the company, and that was exciting.

In addition to deals, Jilliene needed accredited investors. One of the things she did that was a little different to get the company off and running and get access to accredited investors was to meet angel investors. Typically, angel investors invest in startups and are, themselves, accredited investors, so they generally have the ability to invest in real estate. She did a lot of pitch competitions not only to raise capital for the company itself at the corporate level, but also because all of those investors could be viable investors on the platform into real estate.

She went through an accelerator which was a technology accelerator. She had zero tech background when she started the company, since her background is all finance and wealth management, but her co-founder, Justin Hughes, had a technology background and was really running the tech side. Jilliene needed to get educated very quickly in technology, angel investing, and venture capital investing because she knew it was going to be expensive to develop the business she wanted to build because of all the investments in tech. Engineering is expensive and she knew building a brand would be a costly proposition, as well. To build a trusted, digitally distributed real estate brand where people met online rather than in person would require capital. She raised a seed round, did about $10 million in transactions, went on to raise a Series A round, and then concluded with about $100 million in transactions before moving on to raising a Series B round.

The seed round was the biggest challenge because Jilliene and her co-founder hadn't launched yet and hadn't even proven they could build their website. She had to raise her first round of money before she even had a company. Jilliene and her co-founder had zero proof that anyone was actually going to give them money on the Internet. She was pitching the theory that people were going to give them $100 million on the Internet, and as the concept had never been tried before, not just not by Jilliene, but by anyone, folk were telling her she was out of her mind. They couldn't imagine that people would part with their money without meeting someone in person and having an individual relationship.

Going forward, Jilliene predicts that there will be more adoption in the industry, meaning that investors will increasingly move from taking a passive interest in real estate investing to being more active. Investors who have been on her platform for three years and haven't made an investment will sooner or later make that decision to invest because they will come to appreciate that what they are looking at is truly legitimate and they'll know they are comfortable being there. She expects that as the industry grows, there will be some consolidation, especially when the next downturn hits. There will inevitably be those platforms and sponsors that will have issues, because that's just natural.

At the end of the day, track record is going to be a huge part of determining which companies do well. Since the inception of RealtyMogul, Jilliene has been attuned to their track record, and therefore they have never done ground-up construction or anything of that nature. Those with the best track records, Jilliene predicts, will be those that survive and flourish through the next cycle.

13

Patch of Land: Jason Fritton

The impetus for Jason Fritton's story wasn't a happy one. He'd been an entrepreneur for a very long time and had built up a company that was very successful. He owned 100 percent of it and was primarily working with the public sector—mostly with the federal government—and his company had grown to nearly $30 million a year in business. Not a bad thing for a sole owner. He was a pretty happy fellow. Jason was a very young guy; this was back in 2004 all the way through to 2008.

He'd worked hard, developing and expanding the business. Then the financial collapse of 2008 happened and Jason, like so many others, lost his company. A lot of the contracts that he had at that point were frozen and he found himself with very few sources of demand and with very few actual customers. They were huge, beautiful customers, but he had very few of them. When the collapse happened, his contracts were some of the first to go and, unfortunately, he had to roll his company down. At that time, he thinks of himself as having been a kind of dumb kid. He thought that the recession was just a temporary correction and that it was going to change. He never imagined that it was going to be the multiyear quagmire that it became. Unfortunately, instead of just rolling things down, closing up shop, taking his assets, and moving on to the next thing, he ended up losing everything. He lost his house and had to sell his car for cash to make payroll.

On top of all that, he ended up with tax obligations that he couldn't pay. Jason was heartbroken—he had spent so much time and put so much work into the business. And now, seemingly overnight, something had come out of left field to destroy it. It was a black swan event. He had to let his staff go, which was very difficult because they were people he cared about and who cared about him. But he had to move on and find another way to make a living.

He shuttered the company and immediately started a new business with his younger brother, Brian. They started brainstorming about the best way to put this new company together and got a nice little bit of seed investment from some investors out in Chicago. It was a cool little company, but it really wasn't a good product-market fit. Jason and Brian gave it their best shot, but it really didn't go anywhere. Even though they had a decent number of customers and were doing a little bit of business, they really couldn't make it sustainable. It didn't work out, so Jason ended up closing that business down around 2010.

To make ends meet, necessity demanded that he take a job. But Jason was and is a true entrepreneur and, having already found something that worked in his history, independence and entrepreneurialism was in his blood. It wasn't easy going back to a cubicle somewhere and working for somebody else, but that's what he had to do to be responsible and make sure he could make ends meet. He did what needed to be done and took a day job.

He was very fortunate to have a great CEO as his immediate supervisor. Jason was director of digital marketing for a good-sized retail company of six hundred stores across the country. He took his knowledge of how to find customers online and translated that to his position. It was a good staff job and he enjoyed it, but, again, he was an entrepreneur. So while Jason was working his day job he was trying to figure out what he could do with the rest of his life. Something that would be satisfying and allow him to follow his dreams. He would sit on his couch with a little yellow scratch pad and jot down a series of free-flowing thoughts of whatever came to mind. The moment he had an idea for what he could do and what kind of business he could build, he'd put pen to paper.

Jason came up with all kinds of ideas, from tiny specialty Amazon stores to "how to trade rain forest land." Indeed, it was from this crazy idea that the concept for Patch of Land would eventually emerge. The original concept started with the idea that everybody wants to feel like they own land, that they have made a mark on this planet. He was going to buy sections of rain forest and parcel it out to the individual crowd purchasers online. He would be selling the idea that people would have their own little patch of land somewhere, while contributing to a good cause. Win-win!

What he quickly discovered was that, even though there was no revenue model in that particular strategy, there was something in the thesis. When he lost his house, that affected him deeply. Jason thought people take for granted the feeling of having their own place. He, himself, was renting in Chicago because he couldn't afford to buy a home even though Chicago was a lot cheaper than where he was then, in Southern California. One of the things he missed the most from his previously successful life was owning a home. He took the concept that he had of getting people together to fund a larger piece of real estate, that is, the rain forests, and adapted it a little. He realized that real estate was a massive market; most people really can't participate in it because to do so required both a good amount of capital and a good amount of experience, time, and the skills necessary to accomplish whatever project they were trying to do with real estate. And, except in very few situations, real estate wasn't cheap, but it could be very lucrative. It was, and is, a very complex industry.

Before any of the crowdfunding regulations were being talked about, late 2010 to early 2011, Jason started to explore available real estate opportunities. He had had an idea to get a bunch of people together to buy real estate in the rain forests, but there was no revenue model, philanthropically speaking, and it was not sustainable. But there was something that was telling him that real estate was a big opportunity; he was certain that there had to be a way to bring people together and make something great happen. He just didn't really know what that was going to look like at the time.

He started thinking about what type of investment opportunities might be available. Jason started going to the many home foreclosure auctions. Every day in the newspaper there were stories about the housing market and the crash that was affecting communities and the effect it was having on families. It was hard to ignore and Jason felt sure there was a link to the possibility of opportunity at the time. He wasn't a real estate guy at all, being much more of a technology guy, but he wanted to see what was available. He even talked to some of those individual brokers out there who, for a certain price, would teach you about real estate while visiting the auctions.

The real estate market in Chicago was basically still in a slump, barely starting to recover but still a very tough market. Jason started going out to the auctions in Chicago to see what was available for sale and how he could potentially invest. He found a huge amount of opportunity but also a very broken and fragmented process. A property became available in his neighborhood at the time—nicer than the home he was renting. It was in a great neighborhood and it was a good house. It had a new roof, new windows, new electric. In short, there was nothing wrong with this property and it was nicer than his current home. The appraisal on it was for around $300,000; it came up for a minimum bid of $20,000 at auction.

Nobody, not a single person made an offer. They were effectively giving away a $300,000 home and yet nobody bid on it because nobody had any money. Of course, there were people at the auctions who had cash, bidding on other properties. Big properties, million-dollar properties, big opportunities that were being sold for a fraction of their value. Those people weren't paying attention to the smaller places that Jason knew to be valuable and underpriced. There was a glut of distressed real estate that was available at the time and that was causing a significant problem in the community. Such properties had broken windows, were covered in graffiti, ignored, and/or abandoned. These "ghost houses" were dragging down everybody else's property value and entire neighborhoods were suffering because of this huge influx of distressed properties going back to the banks.

Ten years after the recession, it had become very difficult to get a mortgage but, pre-financial crisis, if you could fog a glass, you could get a mortgage on a home. Banks were extravagant in their lending practices and so, when the market collapsed, they had massive lending that was poorly underwritten. The result was a moratorium on lending while banks dealt with all the bad debt on the books. Jason realized that here was an opportunity. All liquidity was completely frozen for almost any type of opportunity, and he saw that even if the market hadn't been just in complete and total disrepair, it was still a very fragmented broken industry. If someone wanted to buy a home at an auction or elsewhere, whether it needed work or not, funding was difficult. Investors had to go out to these shadowy hard moneylenders who were very opaque and hyperlocal. The vast majority of all money for these projects was financed by hard moneylenders within a 50-mile radius of the property itself.

As Jason was searching through this highly fragmented market, he returned to the idea he had thought of earlier—to bring a bunch of people together and make these types of projects happen again. He figured that there were contractors with the experience and the skill set that people with money don't necessarily have and, that by bringing them together, he could tap into their mental and experiential resources as well. What was desperately needed, however, were the financial resources to make these projects happen.

Digging deeper into this idea, Jason started to talk to some legal mentors and startup advisors in the Chicago area. He wanted to validate his idea because one of the big pitfalls of being an entrepreneur is that sometimes things that make perfect sense in one's own head may not translate to real world value. The entrepreneur can end up looking at an idea too closely, be biased, and miss the obvious pitfalls.

He wanted to validate, from the get-go, his general concept. Jason wanted to find all the people who believed there was a good opportunity, get them together in a coordinated and focused way, make these properties nice again, and return them back to the community for a profit. The thesis was sound because it was not only a lucrative investment; it was based on the premise that investors could do good and make money at the same time.

He brought the idea to his mentors and told them what he wanted to do. He told them that there were thousands and thousands of these types of properties out there that nobody was funding, so there was clearly a need. If he didn't do it, these properties were going to be abandoned. People—investors in the community—he told his mentors—wanted to be involved in real estate because they also understood that with the massive crash, there was also an opportunity to invest once the economy started to come back. However, most folk didn't have the access to this asset class or this type of product.

His advisors listened carefully and told him that he had a great idea. They loved his idea and saw a lot of opportunity for it. But that if he did it, he was going to go to prison. The Securities Act of 1933 had prohibited general solicitation in the manner he was proposing for almost 80 years.

This was in early 2011, fully a year before the JOBS Act was passed and before it was even being talked about in Washington. But the Securities Act of 1933 irked Jason. It seemed to be nothing more than an artificial gate preventing him from seizing a great opportunity. And if there was this artificial gate to making something happen, he reasoned, he had to find a key to get the gate opened.

Jason thought of himself as being a very stubborn person. He looked at how he could create an opportunity in an open and public way, giving formerly unavailable access to many people. He discovered that Congressmen

McHenry and Dole were co-sponsoring what became the crowdfunding exemption for the 2012 JOBS Act. It was encouraging for Jason because the idea was getting good reception back at a time when Congress was not working well at all. This JOBS Act was creating a lot of interest on both sides of the aisle. The Republicans really loved it because it allowed for a less regulated way of raising startup capital. That was how it was originally being looked at—to support the small businesses that are the lifeblood of the economy and that were finding it particularly difficult to raise capital. It was a way to be able to do that and allow people to have more control over their ability to invest their own money, which resonated with a certain crowd. The Democrats promoted it because it was the idea of being able to have the community reinvest within itself and to be able to help a traditionally underrepresented and unconnected segment of the population at the same time.

When he found out that there was political momentum building and that this thing could happen, Jason started to light up the phones. He didn't get into any sort of official lobbying, but he did make sure that he reached out to every congressperson that he could find. He wanted widespread support and the opportunity to talk about a case study that he was looking at that would ensure this thing could actually happen. Impetus and interest grew, and when then President Obama indicated his willingness to sign the bill, that's when it all became real. It was at that point that Jason put together Patch of Land as an actual entity.

He put it together in an incubator space, brand new at the time, at the Merchandise Mart in Chicago. He still had his day job and would work that from seven or eight in the morning until six or seven at night, then take the train to the Merchandise Mart. He'd work there until the last train, go home, and do it all over again the next day. And the next.

He started talking to his younger brother, Brian. Jason recognized Brian as an incredibly talented and gifted engineer. Jason knew his brother could play a critical role because he was building what was primarily a technology-focused platform. When speaking of Brian, Jason says he is a bit more prudent and a lot more cautious than he is. Jason had to prove the concept to him over several months and sketch out a business plan. They put together a lean canvas and looked at what the minimum viable product would be. Finally, Jason was able to convince Brian to come on board and that was when they started to assemble the team. Initially, a lot of what they were doing was pitching and, like all startups, it was just very much abstract than real. The team was basically helping to develop the marketing materials and to sketch out how the technology would look.

At the time they were totally self-funded. They had no income and didn't have a business. They were just building the platform and fleshing out the idea. What gave Jason the confidence to persevere with the idea was an unusual combination of making sense within his own mind, being able to see the opportunity potential, and a healthy delusion of grandeur that he could make this thing work. Jason believed that to be successful, an entrepreneur had to be a little bit crazy when starting a company. Something like 80 percent of all startups fail within the first two years. He knew that if local service-oriented startups (landscaping, pizzeria, handyman, etc.) were filtered out of the statistics and one included only those companies that wanted to exist on a national or international platform, then those numbers are closer to a 90 percent failure rate. He knew that if he was going to put everything he had, all his energy and time, his body and soul into making this thing happen, that it only had a 1 percent chance of success. He knew it was a little delusional and that there was a fine line between insanity and genius, so he figured he must be well into the insane part of the equation because he was willing to take the risk.

It was unclear if the JOBS Act would pass and, when it did in 2012, the rules weren't made known for another two years. Jason wondered if it could happen in the first place, and so the team started putting together Plans A, B, and C just in case for whatever reason the legislation fell through or manifest in a way that they had not predicted. One thing he knew for certain was that Patch of Land was going to happen, and that he was going to make it happen. It wasn't a question of whether or not Patch of Land was going to happen. It was simply what form it was going to take.

They started building the platform and putting the technology together. What they built then would go through a number of evolutionary phases. Originally, the business plan called for very much an equity play. They were going to focus on Chicago real estate and Jason started talking to all the aldermen in the city and to the Cook County Land Bank, about getting access to some of the abandoned properties. That took up a lot of Jason's time. In the meantime, Brian and the team were developing both marketing materials and the technology platform. Press began to build; this was an interesting concept.

Things began to snowball. The business became known as one of the early opportunities for the innovative and upcoming real estate crowdfunding industry. Jason was negotiating with a billionaire out of Northern California who might provide some seed funding for this platform when, in late 2012, he got an unexpected call from someone who became his third co-founder—Carlo Tabibi and the Tabibi family. They, too, had taken a look at the opportunity and had done some investing in Lending Club: a US peer-to-peer lending company, headquartered in San Francisco, California. They understood what the opportunity was, and they reached out and offered Jason the prospect of a move to Los Angeles (LA) in return for a few hundred thousand dollars of seed capital.

At this point Jason and his team had not executed on a single deal and were still purely at the conceptual stage. Everything was detailed on a whiteboard; there was a business plan and a platform and a function well in hand. The team were able to do a good demo of what the plan looked like. Jason was conscious that he and his team were primarily technology and not real estate guys; Carlo brought the real estate experience that they needed. He had done private money lending on more than $100 million worth of properties and knew a lot more than Jason's team did about real estate. Deciding not to go with the billionaire guy, who would have been a very powerful resource but very detached, more of an investor than a co-founder, Jason decided to take Carlo's offer and relocate to LA.

At the same time, they switched gears a little bit because they didn't want to be pigeonholed in the Chicago area. There was only so far you could go with that and Jason figured that, if he was going to try and make this thing work, he might as well go big. He wanted to be national and he figured that would be tough to do with an equity play unless he really had the time to analyze all the different opportunities. Realistically all he wanted to do was to provide capital to real estate professionals and be able to give access to a crowd of folk who wanted access to currently unavailable lending opportunities. Providing debt, Jason and his partners decided, would be a much more viable route.

Keeping focused firmly on how the pending regulations would map out, Jason's team began to plan ways to accommodate the new rules, regardless of whether they had a debt or equity platform. The key was that they wanted to raise capital through public solicitation. Under no circumstances did they want to run afoul of the SEC, so they started concentrating on how to build the infrastructure to ensure that they were absolutely compliant. The regulations were critical to Patch of Land because the only way they were going to be able to openly solicit investors on the Internet, in any kind of automated way, was to have these JOBS Act exemptions in place.

Jason drew a lot of influence from sites like Lending Club and Prosper. In fact, the past president of Prosper, Ron Suber, ended up becoming an investor in Patch of Land. Jason also drew inspiration and hope from the success of some of the other early crowdfund real estate players. Jilliene Helman with RealtyMogul had gone through a TechStars program and was winning awards everywhere for the concept. She was raising a lot of money and helped to bring awareness to the industry. Jason still believes that had it not been for

Jilliene and others like her, out there building awareness, it would have been much more difficult for him both to interest Carlo and to interest the eventual crowdfunding investors whom he would need to attract to get started. Here was the real trick—the only way to fund a property would be to have investors give them money. But how to get investors to give money if he didn't have a property or a project?

Patch of Land did their first deal in late September 2013, within weeks of the new regulations going into effect. They had set up everything in preparation and had been counting down to the promulgation of the rules in an effort to be ready to act as soon as possible. Jason knew he had to act quickly. The projects they were working on, fix-and-flip loans to developers, were very high-response projects; meaning these real estate developers might only have a project for a couple of weeks before it would go away and be sold to someone else. They had to get funded within that timeframe. There was a lot of juggling that had to happen to be able to find the right project at the right time to be able to launch and that was dependent upon the actual timing of the promulgation of the regulations. They knew what that date was going to be, so it was a little bit easier to start planning that out.

Jason and his brother arrived in LA with Brian and immediately set about searching for a deal. Although not being a real estate guy, Jason started off by going to real estate agents and brokers and pitching his concept. The professionals they were working with had to know how the money was coming in and what the chances were of the deal closing and Jason wasn't even sure if he could fund the first project and wanted to be forthright with everyone.

At the beginning, there were dozens of opportunities. There were some fix-and-flippers who would have loved to work with them, but they probably weren't as safe as they could have been. For his first deal especially, Jason needed to make sure that his project was a success. If the first project failed, then the whole plan would fail. He knew he wouldn't get a second chance. He needed to make sure that the first deal was as near to a walkover as possible: ready to go at exactly the time he needed to launch. That was a difficult thing to do, so the team went through dozens of different projects.

One deal they were working on came very close but fell through late in the process. It turned out that the attorney who was representing the borrower on the project did his own projects. He was president of a real estate club of high-net-worth individuals and was head of an attorney's office that employed a dozen-plus attorneys. They had a small deal that they were planning on self-funding themselves and agreed to let Jason try to fund it through his platform because, even if there were hiccups in the process, they could handle it and bring in the capital. Jason went out and took pictures of the property and got an appraisal and arranged to close the property with Carlo's capital—essentially pre-fund the property, wait until the regulations go into effect, and then launch it on the website to his crowd investors.

Jason and his team had no idea how many people there might be who would want to invest. They had been testing the waters pre-launch to bring people in and get indications of interest. Jason figured it was probably going to be a lot like a gym membership. Lots of people might sign up, but very few people actually work out or, in his case, actually invest. Jason and his team were worried and expected that, once the platform was launched, they were really going to have to hustle to finance this little $100,000 deal. They didn't have a whole lot of confidence and figured that it would take them at least a month to be able to fund. How many people, he wondered, would actually send thousands of dollars at the click of a button to somebody they had never met before. They launched the deal right before they jumped in the car to go speak at a Las Vegas conference on this new crowdfunding industry. By the time they arrived, the deal had already been half-funded. It was completely funded within a matter of hours. "Incredible," Jason recalls, but this also caused its own problems.

The key thing with e-commerce is to have product to keep people coming back. Jason needed momentum and didn't want to be dead in the water, with no new deals to invest in. All he and his team could do was pitch investors through their site and continue to promise that there were more to come. The whole time he was in Vegas, Jason worked on finding the next property. He was aware that there was always a delicate balance of making sure that he could onboard good projects quickly while remaining safe and ethical. It was tough at first. Patch of Land did one more project relatively quickly and then went an entire month without having another project; again, it did one more and then another month went by without a project. For a while the platform went months at a time with no deals on the site.

It was really challenging in the beginning, but having closed their first deal gave them the confidence to go and line up a bunch of different things. They had the ability to increase their marketing to the borrowers, brokers, and real estate agents directly and to start piling up the projects, while at the same time trawling for investors. The business seesawed between having far too much money to be able to put to use for the number of projects they had and too many projects with not enough money.

Since that time, it has been difficult making sure Jason and his team have a really good buffer on both sides, so they can fund everything that deserves to get funded while, at the same time, not having a whole lot of cash dragging and waiting for an opportunity. That's been part of the evolution of the company. It's been an exciting growth over five years. Jason and his team started with that one little property in one state and, at time of writing, having a 40-state presence, becoming the fifth largest company of its type in the country. No one can argue with the success of a business that has loaned nearly $1 billion.

14

Small Change: Eve Picker

Eve Picker has not had a straightforward career, having taken a very circuitous route to being one of the leaders in the real estate crowdfunding world. An architect by training, she received her architecture degree in Australia, where she became fascinated by the structure of cities. She was accepted at Columbia University in New York, where she studied for a master's in urban design, which is a little bit different than urban planning.

When she was at Columbia everyone was an architect, and it was assumed that they all knew how to build buildings. The one-year program was about understanding how buildings shape public spaces; it was mind-altering for

Eve. It changed the way she looked at things, as did the experience of living in New York City. She stayed and worked there for a while and then her husband, who had tagged along with her from Australia, was invited to Pittsburgh for a year as a visiting fellow in his field. They only planned on being in Pittsburgh for the year, but when her husband was offered a full-time position, they decided to stay.

In her early years in Pittsburgh Eve worked in an architect's office, but really didn't like it very much. At some point she and her husband decided they wanted to buy a house. They had a young child and were living in a rental apartment. They found a neighborhood that had the most amazingly charming houses in it, so they bought a house, moved in, and started renovating it, even though the neighborhood was pretty decrepit.

They didn't know very much about the history of Pittsburgh at the time, and Eve didn't realize they had moved there at a point in time when the city had lost more than half of its population. They came from Sydney, Australia, which is a booming city growing all the time, so this neighborhood they moved into in Pittsburgh looked like a good opportunity for them. But actually it was a neighborhood in decline, primarily driven by mass transit out of the city.

She became active in the community and then at some point heard that a house was being torn down in her neighborhood by a car dealer, who wanted to encroach into the residential neighborhood with a car lot. As an architect, she cared about physical space and buildings and it was a beautiful building that was being torn down, so she found herself picketing on the street with a bunch of neighbors who she had never met before. Out of that event a community development organization was developed with the purpose of rebuilding the neighborhood. Eve was one of its founding members.

At the time, Eve had no idea what a community development organization was, or that they even existed, or what nonprofits did. She knew none of that. She was a novice, but ten years as a volunteer with that organization really taught her everything she knows about building projects in less-than-ideal markets. Pittsburgh has been, for a very long time, a less-than-ideal market. A very soft market. You have to be extremely creative when you're doing real estate there to make the numbers work, and you have to be patient and willing to wait a long time to really get a return. That might be changing now, but that's certainly the way it was when Eve got started.

Complicated Finance

Eve became aware of the complexities of financing real estate when she got involved in a project that was incredibly challenging to finance. Working at the nonprofit taught her a lot about Pittsburgh and about doing the most difficult types of real estate development with public funds. She had gone to work for the planning department, which she found was a pretty amazing job and where she felt the pulse of the city; it inspired her to do her own real estate developments. She didn't love being an architect, so she started to buy buildings and renovate them and turn them to good use.

That's how she fell into development. For Eve, moving to Pittsburgh put her on a path she would never otherwise have been on in any another place, certainly not had she stayed in New York City or in Sydney. But in Pittsburgh, she had an opportunity to think carefully about what projects she was going to take on and what change they might make, and that really mattered to her.

Eve is not driven as a developer to do deals just for the deal's sake. Instead, she is driven as a developer because of the way she looks at cities and because of the way she was trained to think about cities. That really matters to her. She started to do her own real estate developments with some small projects in her immediate neighborhood. It wasn't long before she found a building in downtown Pittsburgh with a big hole in the roof that had been vacant for many years. She converted it into condominium lofts: the first loft project in downtown Pittsburgh.

Bankers thought she was crazy, but when she held an open house, people were lined up around the block to come in and look at it. She sold the project faster than she could build it. There were only eight units, but they were sold immediately. Eve felt like she had tapped into something that people who lived in Pittsburgh didn't quite understand, and she went on to do a bunch of other projects, many of them requiring odd bits of financing that she scraped up in patchwork ways. Eve's real estate financing model never included equity investors because the projects she pursued were such a long haul that she couldn't really show investors what return they would get.

Investors would have to be extremely patient, so Eve would go to the Urban Redevelopment Authority (URA) or other similar sources of funds to look for matching grants or she would use historic tax credits. Anything she could do to make the capital stack work. At the time, the URA she worked with had a very good relationship with local banks, which were also receptive to what Eve was doing. At the time, in the late 1990s, there were 15,000 banks in America, but by the time the JOBS Act was passed there were fewer than 5000. When Eve was first doing these types of developments community banking was alive and kicking, but over the years, it all but evaporated. In addition to bank introductions, the URA did things to help the capital stack to encourage development in these neighborhoods, such as requiring only 5 percent equity participation. Consequently, Eve was able to build a portfolio on sweat equity with a little bit of cash turned in, even though the deals and the capital stack were very complicated. But it was the formula she employed, and it worked well.

Here is what happened in the evolution of things. The Bush administration cut back pretty severely on a source of funds that the local redevelopment authority in Pittsburgh and others nationwide would repurpose for developer loans. These were called Community Development Block Grants. When that source of money dried up in the early-to-mid-2000s, Eve found herself going to the URA with project ideas and they started to say that they couldn't help any longer because they didn't have any money. They lost their funding stream and, as a result, Eve lost her partner and was not able to pull her projects together anymore.

Then, of course the banking crash of 2007–2008 didn't help because banks became more and more conservative about what they would do, and Eve found that her formula for real estate development was no longer tenable. She decided she was going to stop trying, and spent a couple of years stabilizing the projects she already had which were still a little bit fragile. She found people to manage her portfolio, and then she purposefully shut down her development and property management companies and thought about giving herself a year to look for something else to do that utilized her skills.

She had no idea what that was going to be.

In early 2013, a business acquaintance introduced Eve to the JOBS Act. She knew absolutely zero about securities law and barely even knew what "SEC," the acronym for the Securities Exchange Commission, stood for. She started researching the Act while she was winding things down with her development company and found it fascinating. She thought there was a possibility here to build something that would provide a financing tool for projects just like the ones she had been struggling with. And that's really where she began, knowing zero.

What interested Eve the most was Regulation CF, which, of course, didn't go live until almost three years after the Act was passed. Eve particularly liked the idea of everyone being able to invest because, after many years of experience in community development in her community, she could see how people were really motivated to contribute to their own neighborhood. If she'd had the crowdfunding tool when she was doing real estate in those neighborhoods, then local people would have been able to invest locally, and it would have been a fabulous thing.

Driven much less by money and wealth than she was by the idea of democratizing opportunity, Eve learnt through her neighborhood work that there are many people like her who want to contribute in some meaningful way. She thought utilizing crowdfunding could be a meaningful way. "Wouldn't it be great," she thought, "if people could raise money for a project through their neighbors?" And it sounded like they might be able to do this by using that part of the JOBS Act called "Regulation Crowdfunding."

Neither she nor anyone around her really knew how difficult it was going to be, but they understood the promise of it.

Even though Regulation CF was conceived and passed with the small business and startup world in mind, real estate is what defines Eve and what she does, and she immediately saw a connection between this new regulation and real estate. Around 2008 she lost her equity partners when the funding from the URA and matching grants disappeared, and she was still thinking in terms of what she could replace that with to do development again. Eve realized one option would be to go to a bunch of wealthy people and ask them to invest in these challenging projects. However, she also knew that these kinds of diamonds in the rough don't necessarily entice your average accredited investor. But she believed they would be of interest to people who lived in cities in neighborhoods like the one she lived in, and it was with that realization that she connected the JOBS Act to real estate. It's where she saw opportunity.

The idea was seeded. Even though Eve already new that startups were difficult, she went into it thinking it would be easier to build than it ended up being. It cost her much more time and money than she ever imagined. She has no intention of backing down from it, but it has been a much more challenging project than any she's ever done before.

When she started, she thought the rules around Regulation CF would be promulgated quickly, but it took a lot longer than expected. She went about building a platform with the idea that it would be very transparent. She spent a lot of time researching other real estate platforms that had emerged as a means for clarifying her own ideas. What she didn't like about them that she wanted to avoid, even though she does not criticize them at all, is that they primarily focused on the accredited investor. Even so, she found the variety of opportunity in the space fascinating. The way she thinks about securities laws is that they are tools to be used in many ways, and that people are incredibly creative with them.

The opportunity Eve saw in the real estate space was that the platforms emerging early on, for the most part, were still very exclusive. Investors had to join as a member in some way, and at minimum show that they were an accredited investor before being permitted to see anything. That wasn't what she had learned from her community development work. Eve is a Pittsburgher in the way she thinks, and she wanted to have an open transparent site where everyone could see the projects and participate in them. That's what she thought from day one, expecting the regulations to come live, and for her site, Small Change, to be ready for it.

Once the site was completed enough and the rules had been promulgated by the SEC, she launched a test case known as The Tiny House. It was in an extremely underserved neighborhood in Garfield, Pittsburgh, and in this first deal, Eve only permitted accredited investors to invest, which, Eve laughs, "was wrong on so many levels." But it worked, and she was able to use it to test her new platform.

Initially, Eve thought of using Regulation CF for her own deals, but there were logistical issues with that. First, all Regulation CF deals have to be run through a funding portal, and at the time, there were none that catered to real estate. Even after setting up her own funding portal, she was precluded from doing her own deals through the portal, as that is prohibited. Having to use someone else's portal would have been ironic.

It wasn't a difficult decision for Eve, therefore, to decide to establish her own funding portal because she was really fascinated and excited by the idea of helping finance other people's projects because it meant doing something bigger than just doing a handful of her own projects. She was totally engaged with the idea, and that's really what she was thinking. She has had a lot of experience looking at projects like that. She thought she could put her experience to use and do something bigger and provide a financing stream for all those projects that ought to happen that banks really don't want to deal with.

She had never even heard the words "funding portal." She just knew that the JOBS Act said there was going to be a regulation of some sort that lets anyone over the age of 18 invest. In fact, no one knew about funding portals until 2015, when the rules were promulgated toward the end of October that year, and this was several years after Eve had begun her pathway to building a marketplace where, ultimately, everyone would be allowed to invest.

When she started working on it in late 2014 there was a lot to learn. She needed to put a team together and was looking for attorneys and all sorts of other things that needed to be put in place to build the platform. She went live with her first offering almost out of desperation. The Tiny House deal was a Regulation D offering conducted toward the middle of 2015 as a trial run.

Toward the end of that offering the regulations for Regulation CF were put out. Eve spent the first half of 2016 reading these new regulations, defining a strategy for how to deal with them electronically, and rebuilding the back end of her site.

She initially tried to work with a white-label vendor to do cash management on the first deal, but ended up deciding that it was not going to be good enough. She spent all of 2016 talking to developers, and building a following at the same time, until submitting to FINRA for membership. But it became very difficult to talk to developers because she didn't really know how long it would take to become a member. By the time she was accepted as a member of FINRA it was mid-October and she had mostly lost that year in building up her developer pool.

As 2017 kicked off, Eve started tackling developer outreach and began building, in earnest, the infrastructure for a very big pipeline. She did several offerings, though not as many as she would have liked, but she was building a pipeline of projects that would take a long time to come to fruition. In 2018 she began to see momentum build in that long, slow process.

While Eve was waiting for the rules to be promulgated, she was constantly looking at her competitors and reading the news to track developments in the new law. There were a couple of things that she read a lot and one was, and remains, her attorney's blog. Mark Roderick was writing really excellent pieces on the state of the regulations that were very useful and informative. The blog was also useful because, at the time, it was squarely focused on crowdfunding, although it has since moved to crypto currencies and become less relevant for Eve. There were other sources of information from which Eve monitored how the Act was rolling out. She went to conferences to learn, and it wasn't long before she was going to conferences to speak. Eve has shifted from being an absolute novice and learning about JOBS Act regulations to now being a recognized expert in what she humbly describes as a "peculiar little area" of securities law.

Small Change is made up of four companies—a holding company and three subsidiaries. One of the subsidiary companies is called NSSC Funding Portal, which is a member of FINRA and a "funding portal." This is how Small Change can do more than just offer Regulation CF offerings, which funding portals are limited to. Then there is a company that builds the technology and licenses it to the funding portal, which is only permitted to do offerings using Regulation CF, and the fourth company can do offerings using the other regulations.

All her companies were set up to utilize JOBS Act regulations. Eve was the first active funding portal to conduct finance for real estate deals, while most of the other funding portals are primarily focused on providing funding for startups and small companies.

To get started, Eve did a number of Regulation D, 506(c) offerings before her first Regulation CF offering in 2017. She financed around five deals, all 506(c), which is one of the regulations that came out of the JOBS Act and permitted her to advertise to anyone, although she could only accept investors who are designated accredited. These investors have to be verified as accredited, but Eve is able to advertise openly to them.

The first deal, the Tiny House, was a $190,000 project for which Eve raised $100,000 to be used as a construction loan. It was a challenging project, similar to the ones she was used to from her days financing her own deals through the URA. The project was in a very underserved neighborhood and the biggest financing challenge was that, when Eve went to do an appraisal, there were no similar properties in the tristate region for the appraiser to use as comparables.

Consequently, as no bank would give a loan unless they had an appraisal and can compare it to three similar projects that had already been built like it, Small Change could not get a construction loan. To fill this gap, the sponsor raised the money as a loan on Small Change instead using Regulation D, 506(c).

Eve wanted to migrate away from the accredited investor world because she had become accustomed to being in the community development world. She was less attuned to the wealth world because it had not been where she had spent most of her life. Eve passionately believes there is great value in letting people participate in improving the neighborhood or city they live in.

People want to participate, and Eve was uncomfortable with the exclusiveness of a small percentage of people controlling what happens. The accredited investor pool is 3 percent of the population, and Eve was driven by a desire to see everybody have a say in their own neighborhood, not just the wealthy. She likes underdogs and has spent a lot of time in neighborhoods where no one wanted to invest. No banks, no developers. Yet she has ended up with a very nice portfolio built in those neighborhoods because she had the foresight to do it. There's value in those places, believes Eve, that the traditional financial institutions and traditional investors do not often see. There's opportunity that isn't being captured, and when the JOBS Act regulations were first being utilized in the real estate industry, Eve was frustrated by what she saw on the real estate platforms that were emerging, and it wasn't just that they were appealing solely to the accredited investor.

Most of them paid no attention to architecture or how their deals were going to affect the cities in which they were located. Most of them were just using buildings as a way to make people money. And that's fundamentally not the way Eve was trained. For her, buildings should make places better and not just be vehicles for wealth creation. Today, there are hundreds of developers coming to Small Change with ideas that are consistent with Eve's community-centric ethos. As investors flock to her site, it reinforces for her that she is not the only one to think this way.

Eve was acutely aware that the JOBS Act and its regulations were not designed for real estate, but rather built around the thesis that only small companies and startups would benefit from the Act. Seeing the rules and using them gave her this awareness. In real estate, you typically don't create a new LLC until you're ready to close on a deal, and then you start with a brand new LLC with absolutely no operating information on it. When you get the check from the crowd you close the deal and the company's operating history begins. But Eve found that some of the regulations are very clearly geared toward businesses that have been operating for a while and that have had operating experience. Real estate startups don't provide much of that information because there is nothing to report. That said, Eve believes that real estate has been a more voluminous consumer of JOBS Act regulations than small business because, in her view, "small buildings are small businesses." It's the same thing, and someone who's a developer is doing what a small business would do in that building—building a business.

Eve understands this because she has run businesses; however, she finds the idea of investing in a business much more difficult to contemplate than investing in real estate. Real estate is where she lives and breathes. She's a trained architect. She loves cities. It's where she wants to spend her life and she likes changing things and making them better. Pittsburgh has been a wonderful journey for Eve because she has been able to learn about something she never expected to learn and didn't even know existed. It's been transformational for her and she's seen Pittsburgh from its worst possible moment to today, when it's really the comeback kid. It's been an extraordinary experience that she's been able to contribute to because she has been able to tackle real estate that no one else wanted to tackle.

When developers started coming to her with their ideas, every one of them was different. "It's just insane, the creativity," Eve marvels. "Many of them come because they're starting out and they can't find enough equity elsewhere." The bank's equity requirements increased dramatically from needing as little as 5 percent when Eve first started, but by the time Regulation CF became law, they were often asking for 25–40 percent equity. If a young developer didn't have enough family and friends to pull that together, or there were other reasons like lack of comparable properties, which meant the bank didn't want to make a loan, then the deal may not happen.

Eve experienced this firsthand. A building she owns on which she wishes she could have done a Regulation CF offering serves as a great example. The building was a beautiful historic building that she redeveloped around four years before the JOBS Act was passed, and she had been renting almost half of it to a growing co-working business that had grown and grown and had built up quite a few locations. They approached Eve right around the time Regulation CF rules were being promulgated and told her that they wanted to take over the entire building as a co-working building.

They wanted it to be their flagship location. They showed her the numbers and explained how they thought they could make her more money. Their proposal was that she hire them as operators, almost like hotel operators, and they would fill the desks for her. It took them a year and a half to put that together. In the meantime, for 12 years Eve had been paying, making mortgage payments on this building without fail on time to her local bank. The building was probably valued at $4 million at the time and Eve had around $1.6 million left in the balance on the loan. She was in a pretty good position and went to the bank to borrow $250,000 on a credit line to expand the co-working tenant into the rest of the space, taking her loan-to-value ratio to just around 47 percent. After messing around for three months, the bank said no because they couldn't appraise the property; they couldn't find anything like it to compare it with. They didn't know what to do with an income stream from desks versus traditional offices.

Frustrated by how crazy this was, Eve found other ways to raise the money. She had to use Regulation D, because as an owner in the building, she could not be involved in a Regulation CF offering on her own platform. This kind of situation is not uncommon—that some piece of funding is missing for some crazy, illogical reason.

At time of writing, Small Change had three live offerings available for investment and one that had been completed, where an architect needed to raise money to satisfy a bank that wanted more equity. This architect had an investor willing to step in with about half of it, so when Eve set about raising the funds for him, she set the minimum goal at the half he needed if he used his existing equity funds, but she set the maximum goal at the whole amount. In the end, Eve raised the entire amount for a project he would not have done otherwise. The project consists of two lots that have been vacant for a very long time in a vibrant neighborhood on which the architect is building houses. The empty lots were an eyesore because they are odd-shaped lots that the architect found and that no one else wanted to build on. Now, two beautiful, affordable houses are being built that will be sold at a price point that's almost unheard of now in New Orleans. And like this, there are many ways that Regulation CF has benefited communities and will continue to do so.

15

Conclusion

Though it was never intended for real estate, the JOBS Act continues to change the way investment and capital formation occurs in the industry. Within the first four years or so since the laws were promulgated, platforms like those described in this book have attracted more than a hundred thousand registered investors, who have capitalized deals with hundreds of millions of dollars of equity. The real estate industry has been the single largest beneficiary of individual sections of the JOBS Act, equaling alone the use of parts of the Act by all other industries combined.

The previous feudal-like system, where only an elite group of landowners and their wealthy friends invested in real estate, forges ahead with the advent of free access via regulatory change and digital communication. The industry has been democratized on two fronts. Anyone can raise capital and anyone can invest within their means. The move from feudalism to democracy has been nothing short of revolutionary for the real estate industry.

Indeed, there are benefits of democratizing something that was previously only available to a select few—sophisticated, very wealthy investors and sophisticated, well-connected entrepreneurs. By breaking down the barriers of something that had previously been out of reach, the invisible hand wields important social benefits, including job creation and greater economic development in easy-to-ignore places.

To benefit from these changes, however, both investors and developers must master previously unknown or undeveloped skills. To be informed, prudent investors who want to mitigate risk must learn the business of real estate; to effectively raise capital online, developers must embrace the digital world and acquire the skills necessary to communicate online. For the market to mature, both of these phenomena must occur.

In the early stages of this new tech-enabled industry of real estate finance, the impact on developers is greater than it is on investors. For investors, the decision to invest in real estate is entirely optional; it is a function of their appetite for risk and desire to diversify into an alternative investment asset class. For developers it is imperative. Why? Because as online investing becomes more mainstream, the usual sources of capital, those discrete private networks, will increasingly be infiltrated by other developers wanting to tap the same sources and who, up until only 2012, were prohibited from doing so.

Additionally, developers with access to crowdfunding will be at a significant competitive advantage during cyclical downturns. Three things happen during downturns:

1. liquidity dries up,
2. supply of product rises, and
3. prices go down.

There are two interested parties in these periods of distress:

1. developers with access to deal flow but insufficient capital to maximize their access advantage, and
2. investors without access who recognize that investment opportunities abound and want in.

Developers who cultivate an online network of investors during the good times will have unlimited access to crowdfunded capital during downturns to take advantage of the opportunities that appear.

This levels the field and, as in any revolution, the goal is equality for all. That said, investors new to real estate must arm themselves so that they become equal partners with those raising capital. History has allowed investors in private groups to become sophisticated and, for the most part, understand the machinations of deal investment. The space that the JOBS Act left in its wake is that a new generation of investors has no historical experience of real estate and little or no understanding of the risks involved. They either fail to heed the constant messaging that past performance is no guarantee of future results or ignore the experts who tell them the risks are high.

Democratization has not reduced the need to be sophisticated. Real estate investment is not a simple game. It is very high risk and, at time of writing, the real estate market has only been on an upward trajectory. For both the developer and the investor, it has been very difficult to go wrong during these first four or five years since the JOBS Act was passed.

Beyond just an ability to effectively assess the scale of risk they are facing, there is another distinction between the experienced and the nonexperienced investor—their ability to mitigate that risk. Private groups of sophisticated investors—those experienced in real estate transactions and represented by professional advisors—demand certain returns, terms and conditions in their agreements with developers that protect their interests when markets turn downward. The structure of the relationship and the way the returns are paid is carefully calculated and balanced with the risks and exposure. Ongoing exposure to real estate's cyclical ups and downs has made the sophisticated investors adept at managing risk and negotiating terms.

The less experienced investor, unfamiliar with the intricacies of these cyclical changes, cannot be expected to fully understand and calculate the risk exposure; they lack historical knowledge of real estate investment. They don't really understand what the risks are and so they miscalculate the value of their capital—selling it to developers for less than it is worth and less than would the sophisticated investor.

From developers' perspectives, this is highly motivational. They are more inclined to raise less costly capital from the crowd, allowing them to be more aggressive on deal underwriting. If the cost of capital is less than it was yesterday, developers can afford to pay more for real estate today. The inherent risk of the deal hasn't changed; the building will still go up and be rented. What has increased, though, is the level of pricing and associated leverage and hence the investment risk has risen.

Furthermore, crowdfund investors look at the deal supply landscape and demand returns that are competitive. The higher the projected returns, the higher the demand for the deal and the more capital will flow to it. In this paradigm, unlike other competitive markets and counter to common economic theory, competition drives pricing up, not down. Combined with the lower cost of capital, the result is an economic bubble dynamic. Real estate investors want deals that promise higher returns than other deals. Developers strain to oblige. They pay increasingly more for deals while, at the same time, predicting competitively high returns. In the markets in which they play, this has an inflationary impact on real estate pricing. Investor protections also suffer as developers insulate themselves from risk by removing the rights and remedies investors might otherwise expect should overoptimistic deal forecasts fail to manifest—with all that can entail.

Everything works just fine when markets are on the rise. In the first four or five years since the passage of the JOBS Act made real estate crowdfunding possible, the real estate market has continued to rise unabated. Yet rising markets mask many errors that are laid bare only when the economy slumps. To quote Warren Buffet, "Only when the tide goes out do you discover who has been swimming naked."

We're all connected via fast-moving financial markets and are equally subjected to boom-and-bust economic cycles. When availability to information is restricted, or when education is overlooked or misinterpreted, those who have the information and experience are able to use information to enrich themselves and to see the swings of the boom-and-bust market go their way and leave everyone else holding the bag.

As this book has described, JOBS Act provisions were oriented to small business. Compared to real estate, business employs far lower leverage. Real estate involves big money in big transactions backed by big debt. It is certainly true that the amount of debt in the corporate sector has increased dramatically since the 1980s because the subsequent generations of financial executives did not remember the lessons of the Great Depression. It is too easy to forget the past and the things that protected one in the past. The amount of leverage in the corporate sector is significantly higher than it was, but lower than in the real estate market. Any time there is significant debt, players are operating in a place where there are supercharged returns and supercharged risks of loss. Real estate, when done with low leverage, is stable and reliable, and probably earns about the same as the stock market. It can be a reliable asset class that is not going to be subject to the extremes of boom-and-bust cycles. But when you add in leverage at the scale that real estate does, there is a risk of busts that far outweigh even the most grandiose of potential returns.

General solicitation—the ability to openly advertise and an important component of the JOBS Act to which much of the success enjoyed by the real estate industry can be assigned—exposes inexperienced investors to an additional layer of risk. Allowing general solicitation enables those who have concentrated amounts of power and access to information the power to push investment opportunities on to those who may or may not have that information. General solicitation is a provision in the Act that is most likely to create problems: attracting people who should never be investing in the offerings. Such people may not understand the offering or are mis-marketed, believing that this is a great opportunity without knowing what they are getting into. Well-intentioned ethical sponsors apply the sophisticated lessons gleaned over

80 years of self-preservation to how they structure deals and the uninformed are encouraged to invest. This is great for some, but the vast majority of people who have a little bit of savings shouldn't be considering this type of investment without careful study. History proves, time and time again, that they will be left holding the (empty) bag when the market cycle turns.

By allowing general solicitation and with the relative relaxation of disclosure requirements, the JOBS Act has taken us back to pre-1933 in some ways. There were then limited disclosure requirements, no income restrictions on who could invest, and allowable general solicitation. That said, the JOBS Act put a stamp of approval on trends that were already happening. The institutionalization of markets and the move away from broadly distributed retail investors that started in the 1970s and 1980s gave rise to the private nonregistered, accredited investor, Regulation D 506 market. This market was already raising very large amounts of capital and the JOBS Act merely catalyzed the acceleration of that trend. What the Act does in real estate is to push more of the capital raising, more of the money that developers need to keep building toward the unsophisticated investor—minus strong regulations and without strong disclosure or reporting requirements.

There are other interesting analogies with the pre-1933 world. The 1929 stock market crash and subsequent Great Depression was a boom-and-bust cycle that had been driven by retail investors and the unrestricted sales of financial products to the man on the street. Of course, the crash was a stock market crash and there were lots of monetary policies connected to the gold standard and money being pulled out of the United States to pay off European war debts. The collapse of the farm economy impacted the banks in 1929 in the same way that commercial and residential lending hurt banks during the 2008 crisis. There were public utility holding companies which were the collateralized debt obligations (CDOs) of their day, that packaged packages of packages, each one layered on each other and that were held on banks' balance sheets. All these things contributed to the Great Depression. Fortunately, the JOBS Act has not taken us that far back.

But there is another big factor. Since the 1970s and 1980s, we've seen the institutionalization of our capital markets. It's not the common man/woman on the street that is heavily invested in the stock market; it is big institutions, such as university endowments or pension funds and the like. The stock market is more institutionalized and the real estate market equally so. The JOBS Act pulls more people into institutionalized markets that are not designed to deal with them. The rules are crafted for institutions; ordinary people face a far greater risk of losing money. There won't be a systemic impact of the Act on capital markets, but to the extent that it becomes increasingly widespread in real estate, it could have significant impact on the consumer's confidence in the reliability of the real estate market and their role in capitalizing it. Losses will appear in places that are completely unpredicted by investors and, for the real estate industry, this is something that demands our attention.

Unsophisticated investors are easily seduced into believing that the market will continue to rise. They are right, of course, it will keep going up—until it goes down. And we have a long history of somebody being left with the burden—that somebody is often the person least able to shoulder the burden. What we learned in 1929 that resulted in the 1933 enactment of protections is that all investors need the basic information and reliability of a marketplace grounded in honest real information and consistent, ongoing reporting to make good decisions. When that does not exist, both the individual and the entire industry are subjected to enormous risk. This is particularly true for the real estate crowdfunding industry. Moving from the revolutionary growth phase to one of stability and maturity will inevitably involve an intervening phase where markets dive, losses are sustained, and trust in the system is dented.

That said, if investors know what they're doing, educate themselves, and invest prudently, there will be continued investment and growth robust enough to ride out inevitable downturns. What it can lead to, though, is the creation of exotic derivatives that rapidly diverge from the core thesis that it is possible to invest in individual deals, over which the individual investor can make a reasoned and informed decision and put decision-making into the hands of those who control the information. The financial market corollary to this was the commercial mortgage-backed securities (CMBS) and CDOs that were created in the run-up to the 2008 recession that eventually impacted the market badly. In these situations, the market ends up far more reliant on a smaller number of people making decisions—people who are pulling in the next layer of investors, who may or may not be well suited to be in the space and who are the ones most likely to lose money because the market is less transparent.

There is considerable cause for optimism however, and it is founded on the caliber and vision of the leaders of this new industry. These are the *Leaders of the Crowd* split, as they are in this book, into two camps: the political, be they advocate or staff, and the entrepreneurial real estate professional. What makes the impact of the JOBS Act on the real estate industry so notable is that the political group never factored real estate into their calculations or imagined it might benefit, and the real estate pros never politicized their visions. Whichever camp they were in, however, they all were and continue to be agents for change. Through their own windows of perception they all saw an opportunity to bring change for the good to the world: the political group formulating and building the engine by which change could happen, and the real estate force taking the driving seat to drive the engine forward. What they all had in common was a desire to disrupt the status quo and, more importantly, they had the gumption and tenacity to effect that change and were driven to improve the general good. They were the vanguards during a time of revolution that will lead the industry through to its next phase of growth.

The real estate story as told in this book is the chronicle of those leaders whose inspiration and vision gave birth to crowdfunding capital in their industry. What has followed in their pioneering wake is a flood of similar platforms and marketplaces, and an entire ecosystem rising from the foundation they built. At time of writing there are 50 or more marketplace platforms where investors can search for deals. Some specialize in industry-specific real estate, others in geographical; some are more credible than others, some have flourished, others have already failed. Each has its own unique angle. A complete and updated list of all active sites can be found at the website LeadersOfTheCrowd.com.

Slowly but surely, real estate crowdfunding is bringing grassroots change to neighborhoods. People, for the first time, are able to influence development in the neighborhoods where they live by investing in local real estate. The feudal-like, institutionally driven real estate landscape, where retail and food chain stores propagated across the nation, making neighborhoods homogenous, is morphing as real estate becomes democratized. Voting with their investment dollars, people are making impactful investments in their own neighborhoods, bringing eclectic uses to old facades and supporting local businesses with not only patronage and loyalty, but investment capital for their buildings also. Historic buildings too have benefited from the new regulations. Those members of the crowd more concerned with preservation than with turning a profit are providing equity capital to developers whose goals are to protect our heritage.

Developers are rising to the occasion, becoming increasingly confident of their ability to venture into the digital marketing world. Many are setting up their own websites to raise capital online, bypassing marketplaces altogether and going directly to the crowd. Furthermore, the Act has ushered in a new era where successful professionals from industries unrelated to real estate are applying their skills to merge real estate with technology. These entrepreneurs also recognize that the multitrillion-dollar world of real estate is ripe for disruption and are applying their prodigious skills to capitalize on the opportunity, while bringing a fresh perspective. Even some of the largest real estate owners and operators in the world have discovered the benefits of taking their offerings to the crowd. While they have all the capital they need from institutional and very-high-net-worth investors, they see crowdfunding, and its goal for impactful investment, as another arrow in their quiver that complements the usual sources.

* * *

Only six years since the Act was passed and four years since laws were promulgated allowing for the crowdfunding of real estate, the growth could only be described as explosive. Moving from the feudal world of pre-JOBS Act, where only the landowners and their wealthy friends had access to real estate deal flow, to the new world of digital marketing and capital formation where everyone can participate is nothing short of a revolution. As with all revolutions, there will be casualties along the way.

The success of the real estate crowdfunding industry is, however, cause for much celebration; possibilities for the future are immense. Some sites have in excess of a hundred thousand registered users; they have raised from and returned to investors hundreds of millions of dollars. These are not trivial achievements for a tech-enabled real estate platform with fewer than four years of operating history. Yet we are just scratching the surface. As significant as a hundred thousand registered users on one site is, it is insignificant compared to the 11 million accredited investors in the United States—of whom fewer than 3 percent have ever actually invested in their capacity as accredited investor. Hundreds of millions of real estate investments raised and returned is just the beginning in an industry over $6 trillion in size where total untapped household wealth exceeds ten times that amount.

Indeed, there are those whose belief in the potential for the industry extends beyond simple disruption of real estate. Some believe that real estate crowdfunding could replace traditional bank lending. Others see a displacement of institutional capital as a first choice for real estate developers seeking equity, where the costs and burden of going to the crowd are so much less onerous.

The future is bright and the long-term future sustainability and continued growth of the real estate crowdfunding industry will be built on a foundation of trust and meaningful investment; it must remain a safe place for investors to put their savings and hopefully generate a measurable, beneficial social or environmental impact alongside a financial return. The leaders in this book, and others like them, are the pioneers who are bringing opportunity and change to the real estate industry. They are the vanguards of the industry and the guardians of that trust.

Glossary

Accredited Investor Some regulations used by crowdfunding real estate sponsors and marketplaces restrict them from accepting funds from people who are not classified as "accredited investors." To be an accredited investor, one must have at least $200,000 of income for the past two years, with a reasonable likelihood of earning the same again in the current year ($300,000 if a married couple), or over $1 million of net worth, not including one's primary residence. This standard has not changed (much) since it was first set in 1982, at which time there were approximately 550,000 accredited investors in the United States. Today there are over 11 million who qualify as being accredited.

Alternative Investment Some people refer to real estate as an "alternative investment" distinct from "traditional investments," which are generally stocks, bonds, and cash.

Capital Any use of the term "capital" in real estate is synonymous with the term "money." It can be used to refer to debt of any kind or equity of any kind, or to both in unison.

Collateralized Debt Obligation (CDO) A structured financial product where cash-flow-generating assets are pooled together, tranched according to their risk profile, and then sold to investors. In the run-up to the Great Recession of 2008–2009, high-risk mortgage products that came to be known as "subprime" loans were skimmed off larger pools of mortgages. The resulting pools, in their entirety high-risk mortgages, were tranched and reclassified relative to each other, resulting in some receiving extremely high ratings consisting solely of subprime mortgages. Having such high ratings, they attracted conservative and institutional investors, creating considerable liquidity. Based as they were on high-risk mortgages but carrying the veneer of being highly rated, they contributed in part to the market's crash.

Debt Used by sponsors to reduce the amount of equity that they need in a project. Debt typically earns interest and takes no share in the profits of a deal—in contrast to equity. However, debt is usually secured by the property itself and has the highest priority when it comes time to be paid back; an institution or private lender to a sponsor who is getting no share of the profit will be the first person to be paid back and will have the greatest rights in the event the project falters. It is, therefore, the lowest risk component of the finance on a deal.

Development The process by which buildings or land are improved by adding value through construction or renovation. Someone who engages in developing real estate is said to be a developer or sponsor, and their projects, the "developments."

Due Diligence The process by which a sponsor will evaluate a project. It is an intensive phase of the development process that involves careful, systematic evaluation of all risks involved, the market, and all costs. It usually culminates in a financial analysis of the project where every assumption has been thoroughly vetted. Investors in crowdfunded deals do not need to do the due diligence themselves (what a relief!). Their role in protecting their interests, however, is to ensure that the sponsor has conducted project due diligence thoroughly by reviewing their work product.

Equity Equity is the money invested in a property that is designated to receive a share of the profits when the property sells or is leased. It is often paid at a minimum interest rate while the property is being developed or improved. This interest rate is called a preferred return. The equity in a transaction is paid back only after the debt is repaid. Consequently, there is a higher risk of nonpayment. The term "equity" can be used synonymously with the term "investment."

Funding Portal Funding portals are a new type of intermediary created by the JOBS Act that are exempt from the requirement to register as a broker but must register with the SEC and are regulated by FINRA (Financial Industry Regulatory Authority). They are online platforms where Regulation Crowdfunding (CF) transactions can take place and where non-accredited investors may also participate. The concept of the funding portal was to create a layer of investor protection through a third party or portal. The portal conducts some basic anti-fraud, money laundering, and terrorism screening on a deal before the public is granted access. These portals provide educational materials to investors but not investment advice; they make available information about entities raising capital, the issuer, but are not compensated based on the sales of securities sold, and though they do not take possession of investor funds or securities, they do facilitate the offer and sale of crowdfunding securities.

General Solicitation The process by which someone wishing to raise capital for their business or real estate deal can openly advertise to the public anywhere across any media. Previously it was primarily restricted only to those entities "going public" through an initial public offering (IPO), a heavily regulated option. The JOBS Act largely deregulated these restrictions; it is now far less onerous to solicit investment from the general public.

Impact Investment Impact investments are investments made with the intention to generate positive, measurable social and environmental impacts alongside a financial return.

Internal Rate of Return (IRR) The internal rate of return (IRR) is a measure of returns on an investment that considers the effect of time and allows comparisons to be made from one deal to another. The IRR is expressed as a percentage, a little like the way interest is expressed on a bank deposit—the average annual percentage return on an investment. However, it allows for very complicated scenarios to be compared.

Investment Property Investment property is any real estate that is purchased with a view to earning income either from rents or through adding value and selling the property at some point in the future. In short, if a piece of real estate is acquired that is geared to creating income or building wealth of some sort, then it is an investment property. One of the only kinds of real estate one might buy into that is not considered investment property is a person's primary residence, though historic preservation may also fall into this category.

Private Equity Fund A private equity fund is a company (of sorts) where the fund managers, a group of real estate professionals, raise money from institutional investors, pension funds, endowments, sovereign wealth funds, or high-net-worth individuals in order to make investments in real estate. These funds often have investment criteria that will include specific investment strategies and types of real estate (value-added hotels, for example, or maybe class-A apartments), and target returns. Private equity funds do not engage in real estate development themselves; they invest with developers directly and manage those investments on behalf of their institutional clients.

Real Estate Investment Trust A real estate investment trust (REIT) builds a portfolio of real estate properties according to its declared investment strategy and sells shares of itself to the public. Traded REITs, those for which there is a market for their shares, are exposed to general stock market volatility, so while they are collateralized by real estate, they behave in many ways similarly to stocks, rather than the underlying real estate upon which they are based.

Regulation A+—JOBS Act Title IV This has been called a "mini-IP" or "IPO light" because it provides simplified access to public markets for small companies. Issuers can raise capital from accredited and non-accredited investors alike. These mini-IPs are considerably less costly, less time-consuming, and require far lower reporting requirements than full IPOs. The regulation allows issuers to raise up to $50 million per year from both accredited and non-accredited investors through general solicitation, including over the Internet.

Regulation Crowdfunding—JOBS Act Title III Regulation Crowdfunding (Regulation CF) is the part of the JOBS Act most commonly associated with the concept of crowdfunding for three reasons; one, its name; two, it was designed to be inexpensive to implement and therefore accessible to the smallest of companies; and, three, it was open to everyone for investment.

Issuers using Regulation CF were originally permitted to raise up to $1 million every 12 months and to invest in any kind of real estate provided it is a direct investment in real estate rather than through a fund vehicle. Although general solicitation, that is, advertising, is permitted, it has to be conducted through a registered funding portal.

Regulation D, Rule 506(c)—JOBS Act Title II This regulation was an upgrade of the old, commonly used 506(b), which permitted sponsors to raise capital from investors with whom they had a pre-existing relationship. Becoming effective in September 2013, 506(c) eliminated the need for a pre-existing relationship—opening the doors to general solicitation or, more simply stated, permitted sponsors to advertise. This change increased the number of investors in any one deal to 2000 (accredited) investors, although some see this as being an artificial ceiling and that the regulations allow for an almost unlimited number of investors. 506(c) continues to require very little disclosure or ongoing reporting, as did its predecessor, although the SEC, in writing the rules following the passing of the Act, added some layers of complexity as to how an investor actually gets verified as being accredited.

Returns Any kind of payment that is made to an investor as a result of an investment in a real estate deal is considered a "return" of some sort. The terms that define this concept include return on investment (ROI), return on equity (ROE), cash on cash, rate of return, yield, and others. Unfortunately while these terms are often used in the industry, their definition is not consistently understood. Be sure to ask if in doubt.

Sponsor The sponsor is the person, or entity, who has taken upon themselves the responsibility of acquiring, developing, renovating, and/or managing a property. The sponsor will typically have full management decision authority and, with that, responsibility for ensuring things progress as planned. Other terms used synonymously with "sponsor" include "developer," "operator," and "principal."

Underwriting This is the process by which the extent of risk in a deal is measured, with a view to making an investment. The term is most often used to describe the process a lender will engage in to decide whether to extend credit to a borrower and, if so, how much.

Index

NUMBERS AND SYMBOLS

1934 Securities Exchange Act, 60

A

Accredited investor, 5, 11, 22, 23, 26, 40, 41, 51, 54, 55, 63, 64, 87, 88, 90, 106, 109–111, 128, 147, 148, 150, 157, 160
AH Capital, 127
Alabama, 52
Alternative investment, 11, 105, 116, 154
Amazon, 133
American Bankers Association (ABA), 47
American Dream, 65
American Jobs Act, 72, 73, 75
Americans for Financial Reform, 32
American Sustainable Business Council, 30, 31
Angels List, 106
Anti-fraud, 60
App, 35, 36, 91
Appraisal, 134, 140, 150
Athwal, Nav, 10, 103–114
Auctions, 133, 134
Australia, 143, 144

B

Baby boomer, 10
Bachus, Spencer (Senator), 46, 52
Bank of Tokyo-Mitsubishi, 125
Banks, 8, 19, 25, 26, 35, 45–47, 49, 55, 58, 63, 88, 95, 106, 111, 116, 125, 127, 134, 145, 146, 148, 150–152, 157, 160
Bay Area, 103
Ben and Jerry's, 28
Bennet, Michael, 78
Best, Jason, 7, 59
Big Bang, 19
Bipartisan, 44, 47, 48, 51, 73, 78, 80
Bipartisan support, 48, 53, 73, 76, 114
Blackrock, 14, 26
Bonds, 1, 11, 116, 125
Boston, 21
Broker, 16, 17, 19–21, 23, 85, 86, 91, 103, 134, 139, 140
Broker dealers, 22, 43, 44, 60, 64, 84–86
Brown, Scott (Senator), 42, 78, 97, 98
Bubble, 41, 155
Buffet, Warren, 62, 156
Bush, George W., 146
Bush-Cheney, 46

C

California, 10, 23, 29, 83–87, 109, 113, 138
Canadian, 83
Cantor, Eric, 53, 77
Capital, 2–4, 7, 8, 10, 12–14, 16, 18–26, 28, 31–36, 38, 42, 43, 48, 51, 54, 56, 58–66, 72, 80, 81, 84, 86–88, 90, 94, 99, 104–113, 118, 122, 125, 128, 133, 136, 138, 139, 145, 146, 153–155, 157, 159, 160
Capital formation, 2–9, 13, 20, 25, 30, 44, 48, 49, 51, 53, 61, 62, 65, 73, 75, 76, 80, 96, 97, 101, 153, 160
Capitol Hill, 37, 45, 53
Carper, Tom (Senator), 50, 51
Cassady-Dorion, Zak, 7
CBRE, 84
Celgene, 14
Certificate of Deposit (CD), 116
Chicago, 132–138
Chile, 44
China, 19, 24, 57
Chopra, Aneesh, 98
Chrysler, 46
Chrysler Financial, 46
Citibank, 15
Clinton, Bill, 74
CNBC, 111
Collateralized debt obligation (CDO), 157, 158
Collect, Clean, Aggregate and Report (CCLEAR), 44
Colorado, 29
Columbia University, 143
Comment letter, 96, 97, 100
Commercial mortgage-backed securities (CMBS), 158
Committee, 38, 39, 46, 52, 58, 77
Community Development Block Grants, 146
Concert Capital, 35
Conference committee, 78
Conflict mineral, 51, 52
Congress, 2, 4, 7, 8, 15, 18, 23–25, 30, 37, 42, 43, 53, 55, 58, 70–73, 75, 77, 78, 93, 136
Connecticut, 29
Cook County Land Bank, 137
Covered security, 97
Craigslist, 121
Crowdfund Capital Advisors, 43
Crowdfunding, 1–5, 9, 11, 22, 23, 25, 28, 40, 41, 44, 50, 58, 60, 63–67, 73–81, 87, 90, 98–100, 112, 114, 116–120, 127, 133, 136, 137, 139, 140, 143, 147, 149, 151, 152, 154, 156, 158–160
Crowdfunding Commonsense Compromise Bill, 39
Crypto, 149
CVS, 34

D

Dallas Cowboys, 108
Debt, 106, 108–110, 120, 122, 134, 138, 156, 157
Delaware, 50
Del Taco, 85
DeMint, Jim, 48
Democratization, 4, 155
Democratized, 64, 80, 101, 153, 159
Democrats, 39, 45, 48, 50, 51, 58, 64, 78, 136
Department of Defense, 71
Department of Veterans Affairs, 71
Developers, 2, 12, 89, 95, 104, 105, 108–112, 139, 145, 146, 149–151, 153–155, 157, 159, 160
Development, 2, 7, 12, 28, 29, 59, 65, 72, 81, 94, 95, 97, 104, 107, 127, 144–150, 153, 159

Digital ads, 86
Digital Communication, 153
Disclosure, 44, 56, 60, 61, 63, 64, 96
Disclosure requirements, 2, 157
Distress, 134, 154
Diversification, 110
Dodd Frank, 25, 47, 52, 72, 99
Domestic Policy Council, 71
Dot Com Bubble, 15, 16, 18, 24
Downturns, 129, 154, 158
Due diligence, 25, 110, 119, 122

E

e-Commerce, 4, 140
Eisenhower Executive Office Building, 70
Ellis Rochkind, Dina, 8, 45
The Entrepreneur Access to Capital Act, 31
Entrepreneurs, 3, 7, 9, 11, 21, 36–39, 44, 74, 76, 79–81, 115, 117, 121, 126, 131, 132, 135, 137, 153, 159
Equity, 10, 14, 15, 19, 43, 75, 76, 78, 84, 85, 95, 98, 109, 110, 120, 122, 137, 138, 145–147, 151–153, 159, 160
E-Trade, 111
Executive Office of the President, 70
Exemptions, 2, 7, 22, 29, 30, 37, 44, 60, 105, 106, 113, 136, 138
Exxon Mobile, 17

F

Facebook, 22, 38, 50, 54, 81, 86, 94, 100, 111
Farella, Braun and Martel, 104
Federal Reserve Journal, 30
Ference, Mike, 53
Financial Industry Regulatory Authority (FINRA), 31, 32, 43, 149
Financial Services Committee, 38

Fix-and-Flip, 11, 106, 111, 120, 139
FLAVORx, 34–36, 55
Florida, 79, 109
Forbes, 5
Form 1A, 96
Form 11, 96
Form S-1, 96
Fortune 500, 34
Fritton, Brian, 132, 136, 137, 139
Fritton, Jason, 11, 131, 132
Funders Club, 106
Funding portal, 8, 12, 32, 42, 43, 60, 61, 148, 149
Fundrise, 10, 90, 100, 101, 107, 112, 113

G

Garfield, 148
Gate Global Impact, 49, 50
Gekas, George (Congressman), 46
Genentech, 13, 14
General Catalyst, 108
General public, 1–5, 10, 23, 36, 38, 62, 96–98, 113
General solicitation, 4, 21, 23, 54, 55, 61, 62, 64, 66, 85, 90, 106, 135, 156, 157
Gilt Group, 50
Glass Steagall Act, 15
Goodwin Procter, 52
Google, 86, 116
Goretex, 50
Gramm, Phil (Congressman), 46
Grant Thornton, 21
Great Depression, 1–3, 15, 25, 26, 156, 157
Great Recession, 1, 3, 9–11, 15, 19, 36, 70, 72, 90, 93, 94, 116, 117
Green, Andy, 8, 57
Greenspan, Alan, 16
Groupon, 94

Index

H

Halaris, Nick, 127
Hard Rock, 113
Hardwick ('Wick') Simmons, 15
Heartland, 20, 21
Hedge fund, 17, 52, 54, 63, 65
Helman, Jilliene, 11, 125, 138
The Hill, 37, 38, 46, 49, 52, 54, 55, 58, 76, 97–99
Hofer, Harold, 9, 10, 83
House of Representatives, 31, 72, 97
Hughes, Justin, 128
Hutchison, Kay Bailey (Senator), 47, 49

I

Impact investment, 160
Incubator, 107, 108, 136
Information Age, 7, 56, 65
Initial public offerings (IPO), 6, 14, 15, 18–22, 24, 35, 48, 49, 51, 61–63, 123
Instagram, 100
Institute for Policy Studies, 27
Intel, 17, 21
Internal rate of return (IRR), 88
Internet, 3, 4, 15–17, 79, 84, 85, 93, 95–97, 101, 115, 119, 126, 128, 138
Intrastate exemption, 29
Investment Company Institute (ICI), 54
Investment property, 119, 122
Investor protection, 8, 31, 47, 53, 56–67, 73, 80, 81, 99, 155
Investors, 2, 5, 7, 10–12, 16–18, 21–23, 26, 29–32, 34–36, 40, 41, 43, 44, 50, 51, 54, 55, 57–67, 73–75, 81, 84–91, 95, 98, 100, 103–113, 115–123, 125–128, 132, 134, 135, 138–140, 145, 147, 148, 150–160
Invisible hand, 153

IPO on-ramp, 40, 51–53, 75–77
Ippolito, Ian, 11, 115–123
Issa, Darrell (Congressman), 30

J

Jen-Hsun Huang, 14
Jiang Zemin (President), 19, 20
JOBS Act, 4–12, 16, 22–26, 31, 32, 39, 41, 42, 47–56, 60–64, 66, 71–75, 77, 78, 80, 81, 84, 85, 87, 88, 90–91, 93, 97, 99, 105, 112–114, 117, 125–127, 135–138, 146–158
JP Morgan, 15

K

Kalil, Tom, 74
Kane Anderson, 35
Kassan, Jenny, 7, 27–32, 37, 74, 81
Katovich, John, 28
Kerrigan, Karen, 37
Kickstarter, 36, 43, 74, 79
Kingdom of Saudi Arabia, 44
Kiva, 36
Koll, 84
K Street, 78

L

Larry Fink, 26
Lending Club, 109, 110, 116, 117, 120, 123, 137, 138
Leverage, 3, 88, 105, 109, 155, 156
Levitt, Arthur, 15–17, 20
Liles, Walton, 52
LinkedIn, 38
Living Social, 94
Lobbyists, 7, 38, 40, 46, 47, 51, 54–56, 78–81
Los Angeles, 65, 83, 110, 126, 127, 138, 139

M

Main Street, 50, 51
Make Magazine, 30
Malibu, 126
McHenry, Patrick (Rep.), 23, 31, 38, 53, 55, 60, 73, 76, 78, 136
Menlo Ventures, 109
Merchandise Mart, 136
Merkley, Jeff (Senator), 8, 58, 59, 61, 64, 78
Mexico, 44
Microcap, 18, 20
Microsoft, 17
Millennials, 9, 10, 89–91
Miller, Ben, 10, 93–101
Miller, George, 50
Mitchell, Kate, 51
Molinari, Vincent, 49, 50
Moretti, Enrico, 23
Morgan Stanley, 15
Mortgage, 55, 65, 134, 152, 158
Mountain View, 107
Multifamily, 89, 104, 108, 109, 119
Murphy, Mark, 50
Mutual funds, 17, 54, 105

N

Nasdaq, 6, 15, 16, 19, 20, 62
National Association of Securities Administrators Association (NASAA), 49
National Economic Council, 71, 72, 74
National Institute of Health, 71
National Security Council, 71
National Venture Capital Association (NVCA), 48, 51
Neiss, Sherwood "Woodie," 7, 8, 30, 33–44, 55, 59, 79, 81, 99
New Jersey, 29
New Orleans, 152
New York, 21, 28, 29, 57, 69, 95, 109, 110, 112, 143–145
New York Stock Exchange, 48, 51, 62, 63

Non-accredited, 35, 50, 51
Non-accredited investor, 66, 84, 85, 87, 88, 90, 106, 112, 113, 118, 122
Nontrade REITs, 85
Northern California, 137
NSSC Funding Portal, 149
NYU Stern School of Business, 14

O

Oakland, 28, 29, 103
Obama, Barack (President), 9, 30, 32, 57–59, 64, 69, 71, 72, 74, 76, 78, 98, 136
Obamacare, 126
Office of Science and Technology Policy (OSTP), 70, 71, 74
On-ramp, 40, 48, 51–54, 75–77
Operators, 105, 108, 112, 113, 152, 159
Orsi, Janelle, 30
Oval Office, 70

P

Pabst Blue Ribbon, 53, 73
The Pacific Stock Exchange, 28
Passive income, 88, 111, 126
Patch of Land, 11, 90, 131–141
Paulson, Hank, 26
Pay per click, 86
Pennsylvania, 45, 46, 50, 51, 55
People's Community Market, 29
PeopleSoft, 34
Philadelphia Chamber of Commerce, 49
Picker, Eve, 12, 143–152
Piketty, Thomas, 32
Pioneers, 4, 6, 12, 88, 160
Pittsburgh, 12, 144–146, 148, 151
Piwowar, Mike, 19
Platform, 5, 10, 12, 36, 41, 43, 49, 50, 60, 61, 64, 74, 84–88, 90, 91, 94, 95, 100, 105–114, 116–122, 127–129, 136–140, 147, 148, 150, 152, 153, 159, 160

Pre-funding, 118, 119, 122
President, 9, 15, 19, 20, 32, 41, 57, 59, 64, 69–73, 75–78, 80, 81, 97, 136, 138, 139
Private markets, 21, 22, 63, 64, 66
Private placement exemption, 106
Prosper, 81, 109, 110, 138
Prudential Securities, 14, 15
Prudential Financial, 15
Public markets, 3, 8, 14–16, 18, 20–22, 24, 33, 34, 53, 63, 64

Q

The Queen, 83

R

Rand, Doug, 9, 30, 40, 41, 69–81
Real estate, 2, 19, 29, 54, 65, 80, 83, 93, 103, 115, 125, 133, 143, 153
Real estate investment trust (REIT), 10, 26, 85–87, 89, 91, 112
RealtyMogul, 11, 90, 107, 112, 113, 125–129, 138
RealtyShares, 10, 90, 103–114
Reg A+, 25, 48–51, 55, 62, 63, 66, 85–90, 99–101, 113, 126
Reg ATS, 19
Reg CF, 7, 8, 12, 23, 41–44, 51–54, 60, 63, 66, 67, 146, 147, 149–152
Reg D, 22, 37, 52, 54, 63, 64, 66, 84, 96, 99, 148, 150, 152, 157
Registered investment advisor, 22
Regulation A+ (JOBS Act Title IV), 25, 48–51, 55, 62, 63, 66, 85–90, 99–101, 113, 126
Regulation Crowdfunding (JOBS Act Title III), 66, 106
Regulation D, Rule 506(b), 113, 127
Regulation D, Rule 506(c), 51–53, 150
Reporting requirements, 2, 120, 157

Republicans, 71–73, 76–78, 136
Returns, 23, 29, 35, 36, 38, 79, 81, 88, 107, 111, 112, 115, 116, 119, 135, 138, 144, 145, 155, 156, 160
Revolution, 6, 154, 159, 160
Revolutionary, 5, 153, 158
Rich Uncles, 9, 10, 83–91
Risk, 2, 14, 25, 30, 50, 53, 58, 59, 61–63, 65, 75, 79, 88, 89, 99, 109, 137, 153–158
RiteAid, 34
Roderick, Mark, 149
Rose Garden, 32, 41, 72, 78, 80, 81, 99
Russian, 58

S

S-11, 87
San Francisco, 21, 35, 58, 104, 110, 112, 138
Sarbanes-Oxley, 24, 75, 76
Sarbanes-Oxley 404 B, 52
Schapiro, Mary, 30
Schumer, Chuck, 51, 52
Schweikert, David (Congressman), 48
Sears Roebuck, 94
Secondary market, 44, 51, 89
SecondMarket, 49, 50
Secretary of the Treasury, 26
Securities Act of 1933, 2, 105, 135
Securities Exchange Commission (SEC), 5, 7, 8, 15–17, 19, 20, 22, 25, 30, 37, 41–43, 49, 52, 53, 55, 60–66, 73, 87, 96–101, 106, 117, 127, 138, 146, 148
Senate, 7, 8, 23, 31, 38, 39, 48–53, 58, 70, 76–78, 80, 97, 98
Senate Banking Committee, 39, 58
Series A, 109, 110, 128
Series B, 112, 128
Series C, 112
Shareholder limits, 8, 47, 49, 50, 52–54, 61

Shareholders, 8, 47, 49, 50, 61, 89
Shell, 100
Shuman, Michael, 27, 28, 30, 32
Silbert, Barry, 49, 50
Silicon Valley, 20, 34, 59, 63, 95, 107
Single-family homes, 103
Small Business Advisory Committee, 52
Small Change, 12, 143–152
Small Company Offering Registration (SCOR) form, 29
Social media, 3, 38, 58, 94, 98, 100
Software, 33, 95
Sophisticated investors, 2, 62, 63, 66, 155
Specter, Arlen, 47
Spinrad, Paul, 30
Sponsors, 5, 8, 10, 23, 38, 54, 60, 87, 88, 90, 105, 109, 110, 117, 120, 121, 129, 150, 156
Startup America, 76, 78
Startup America Legislative Agenda, 76, 77
Startup pitch competition, 36
Startups, 4, 7, 19, 20, 22, 34, 35, 38, 50, 72, 74, 77, 79, 80, 107, 115, 117, 121, 126, 128, 135, 147, 149, 151
State of the Union, 72
Stein, Kara (Commissioner), 62, 64, 65
Stocks, 1–3, 11, 13, 15–21, 63, 91, 105, 111, 112, 116, 125, 156, 157
Student housing, 86, 89
Subcommittee on Capital Markets, 24
Subcommittee on Economic Policy, 48
Suber, Ron, 138
Summit Capital, 35
Super Bowl, 64
Sustainable Economies Law Center (SELC), 30
Sydney, 144, 145
Syndicates, 1, 2, 4

T
Tabibi, Carlo, 137
Tea Party, 47, 48
Tech, 4, 5, 9–11, 31, 74, 86, 87, 95, 128
Technology, 5, 23, 33, 34, 36, 42, 59, 60, 64, 65, 70, 71, 74, 84, 94, 103, 105, 106, 112, 127, 128, 134, 136–138, 149, 159
TechStars, 138
Tester, Jon (Senator), 48, 51, 55
Texas, 84, 85, 91, 108, 109
Thalidomide, 14
Thunderbird, 33
Tick, 6, 7, 14, 16–20, 24
Times Square, 95
The Tiny House, 148, 150
Title I, 25, 48, 61
Title II, 106, 113
Title III, 66, 67, 105
Toomey, Pat (Senator), 8, 46–51, 53, 55
Toomey-Carper, 50
Treasury Department, 34, 46, 51, 75
Triple net, 88, 89
Trust, 18, 26, 59, 61, 94, 95, 101, 107, 108, 117, 128, 158, 160
Twitter, 38, 50, 100

U
UC Berkeley, 104
UCLA, 83
Underwriting, 108, 110, 118, 121, 122, 155
Unintended consequences, 6, 17, 26, 59, 80
Union Bank, 125
Union Square Ventures, 112
University of California at Berkeley, 23
Urban Redevelopment Authority (URA), 145–147
US Treasury, 26

V

Vanguards, 5, 159, 160
Vegas, 140
Venture capital, 10, 20, 21, 48, 51, 63, 86, 108, 118, 128
Vermont, 28
Vworker, 115

W

Walgreens, 34
Wall Street, 7, 13, 14, 17, 19, 28, 32, 33, 51, 54
The Wall Street Journal, 47
Washington, 4, 6, 7, 9, 38, 40, 43, 79, 80, 135
Wawa, 49–51
Web traffic, 86
Wefunder, 97, 99
Wegman's, 50, 51
Weild and Co., 25
Weild IV, David, 6, 13–26
The West Wing (TV series), 71
White House, 7–9, 30, 40, 41, 48, 52, 59, 69–81
White House Counsel, 71
White, Mary Jo, 42, 64
Wirta, Ray, 10, 84
WL Gore, 50, 51

Y

Yahoo News, 111
Yale, 14, 27

Z

Zuckerberg, Mark, 22

Printed by Printforce, the Netherlands